SRA
Content Connections
Level B2

 SRA

Columbus, OH

Corrective Reading Content Connections Level B2

Grateful acknowledgement is given to the following publishers and copyright owners for permissions granted to reprint selections from their publications. All possible care has been taken to trace ownership and secure permission for each selection included. In case of any errors or omissions, the Publisher will be pleased to make suitable acknowledgements in future editions.

Reprinted from COME ON SEABISCUIT! By Ralph Moody by permission of the University of Nebraska Press.

"Fabien Cousteau on Swimming with Sharks", Weekend All Things Considered, December 3, 2005. Copyright 2005 National Public Radio. Used by permission.

Reprinted with the permission of Simon & Schuster Books for Young Readers, an imprint of Simon & Schuster Children's Publishing Division from A PELICAN SWALLOWED MY HEAD AND OTHER ZOO STORIES by Edward R. Ricciuti. Text copyright © 2002 Wildlife Conservation Society.

"Goldiefox and the Three Chickens" from LEAPING BEAUTY by GREGORY MAGUIRE. Used by permission of HarperCollins Publishers.

"'Clemente' Tells the Story of a True Baseball Hero", Weekend Edition Sunday April 30, 2006. Copyright 2006 National Public Radio. Used by permission.

Reprinted with the permission of Simon & Schuster Books for Young Readers, an imprint of Simon & Schuster Children's Publishing Division from THE GOOD GUYS OF BASEBALL by Terry Egan, Stan Friedmann and Mike Levine. Copyright © 1997 Terry Egan, Stan Friedmann and Mike Levine.

Cutaway: The World Series, "Remembering My Youth, Through Baseball" News & Notes, October 21, 2005. Copyright 2005 National Public Radio. Used by permission.

SRAonline.com

 SRA

Send all inquiries to this address:
SRA/McGraw-Hill
4400 Easton Commons
Columbus, OH 43219

ISBN: 978-0-07-611263-0
MHID: 0-07-611263-2

3 4 5 6 7 8 9 DOW/ROV 13 12 11 10

The McGraw-Hill Companies

Contents

Read Aloud to All Students

It's no secret that reading aloud to children is the most important thing adults can do to prepare children to be good readers. After evaluating over 10,000 research projects, the Commission on Reading reported in *Becoming a Nation of Readers,* "The single most important activity for building the knowledge required for eventual success in reading is reading aloud to children. . . . It is a practice that should continue throughout the grades."

We also know that in our society, non-readers are seriously handicapped. Successful people read because they have to and because they want to. When you read aloud to your students, you

- Model enthusiasm for reading.
- Model qualities of good reading.
- Provide a role model.
- Build warm, positive relationships with your students.
- Build listening skills, vocabulary, memory, and language skills.
- Provide opportunities to explore social, moral, and ethical issues.
- Develop knowledge bases.
- Encourage abstract thinking and reasoning skills.
- Challenge students to think beyond their own limited experiences and ideas.
- Open lives to boundless opportunities.

There are five or six basic organizers and many variations of each of them. Two of the most effective ways to help students develop comprehension skills are to model thinking strategies and show them how to use graphic organizers. Perhaps you remember a teacher who gave you vague, unhelpful hints to find the main ideas and supporting details. And you were thinking, "I wouldn't know a main idea if it bit me. Can't you take the time to show me what to look for? Can't you take the time to validate my ideas or show me a better way?"

If you want to concentrate on teaching thinking strategies and using graphic organizers, doing that in a read-aloud situation eliminates a huge obstacle. It allows the students to focus on the thinking processes without having to worry about decoding. And once students have good tools for thinking and comprehending, all of the reading processes seem to work together more easily.

Strategies for Comprehension

Of course, not everyone has the same ideas, and lots of things may color our thinking. The ways we get to answers and ideas are different depending on our experiences, our knowledge base, and our view of the world. However, when you can explain to another person how you got to an idea, you clarify it for yourself. You can also help the other person become aware of the thinking processes and help him or her develop strategies for processing information.

For example, you can develop strategies for distinguishing between fact and opinion. There are facts, opinions, lies, and all manners of misinformation—and all kinds of things in between. And it's important to know the difference. So, when you're reading a "factual" article in a magazine, you might read a statement and think, "We define a fact as something that is true, and there is at least one way to prove that it's true. Is there any way to prove this statement is true? That it is a fact? I can look up information from reliable sources. I can talk to an expert about it. I can experience it for myself. I can talk to a reliable source who has experienced it." Opinions can be feelings, beliefs, views, or convictions. At the simplest level, they're easy to recognize:

"Mushrooms are yucky."

"Well, that's your opinion—you can't prove that they're yucky, and I like them."

However, views, beliefs, and convictions can be more complicated to spot. We've expressed a lot of views in this introduction, and you can probably identify them, but can your students? So, that's why we suggest you teach thinking strategies.

Use Graphic Organizers

Most minds understand some things more clearly with a graphic or verbal illustration. "I don't understand. Draw me a picture. I need a map." We tell stories to illustrate a belief or conviction. We draw diagrams to clarify the operation of a gas-powered motor. We use circles and squares and connecting lines to illustrate relationships. Graphic organizers are tools for expressing ideas and clarifying information.

There are five or six basic organizers that are used with primary, elementary, and middle school students, and there are many variations of each of them.

Comparative maps are excellent for showing similarities and differences. One of the most popular is the Venn diagram. Generally, Venn diagrams are shown with two overlapping circles. More than three becomes too cumbersome to deal with. Tables or matrices also work well for comparisons and contrasts.

Story Maps or Story Plot Maps can be conveyed in writing or with drawings, depending on the abilities of your students. These maps help students identify either the main events in the story or the elements of story.

Thematic Maps are used to show main ideas and supporting details. Spider Maps are used when there is not a hierarchy of ideas. Network Trees are used when there is a hierarchy.

Continuums, such as timelines or scales from high to low, are effective for organizing information on a scale from first to last, high to low, or more to less.

Series of Events Maps help organize information in steps or stages. These maps can be chains of events, steps on a ladder, cycle maps, or outlines.

Graphic organizers are suggested for the selections in this anthology. Often more than one type will work, or you might prefer to use organizers of your own. Use what works best for your situation.

Lesson Map

There are four fiction and eight non-fiction selections in the anthology. You may use the selections at any time and in any order. The suggested format for read-aloud lessons is:

1. Getting Started.

2. Read the selection to the group.

3. Present the graphic organizer.

4. Read the selection to the group while working with them to use the graphic organizer.

5. Assess understanding.

Getting Started provides a little background information and targets a few vocabulary words the students will need to know as they're listening.

Read the selection to the group. The first reading should be presented with minimal interruption. If a student does ask a question, answer it and continue reading.

Present the graphic organizer. Display the graphic organizer, and explain how the organizer can help the students understand and remember what they read or hear. Explain to the students that they will work through the organizer with you.

Read the selection to the group while working with them to use the graphic organizer. Reread the selection in sections, and ask questions that will help the students develop thinking skills. Suggestions are with the selection. The suggestions are simply a place to begin. If necessary, model the thinking process. Write the information on your organizer.

Assess understanding. Distribute copies of the graphic organizer. Tell the students to listen to the selection again and make notes on the graphic organizer. Reread the selection for the students.

Also included in the lesson plan are a list of Web sites that will have additional information, visuals, and audio experiences that will provide additional opportunities for listening and using organizers.

Animals

Baker's Bluejay Yarn

FICTION

LESSON MAP

1. Getting Started.
2. Read the selection to the group.
3. Present the graphic organizer.
4. Read the selection to the group while working with them to use the graphic organizer.
5. Assess understanding.

MATERIALS

- Graphic Organizer #1—Story Elements: displayed on an overhead; a copy for each student
- Related Web sites:
  http://www.marktwainhouse.org/
  http://www.twainquotes.com/
  http://www.pbs.org/marktwain/
  http://www.marktwainmuseum.org/

1 Getting Started

BACKGROUND

1. "Baker's Bluejay Yarn" is from Mark Twain's book *A Tramp Abroad*. It is Twain's unique style of nonfiction—a fabricated story with fabricated characters wrapped affectionately around truth. Although Twain laughs at himself and at others, his isn't a mean humor, and it is liberally spiced with wisdom.

2. The narrator of the book is an American tourist traveling through Germany and the Alps with his friend Harris. This story is a tall tale about a bluejay.

VOCABULARY

Present the vocabulary words, using this format:

Scold is a verb that means **chew out, tell off.** What is **scold?** *Scold is a verb that means chew out, tell off.*

Listen. **The bluejay darted above the cat, giving it a good scolding.** Say that. *The bluejay darted above the cat, giving it a good scolding.*

reckon *verb,* imagine, guess, think. *I reckon he thought this was a perfect place to live.*

confound it expression indicating frustration. *Confound it, I don't seem to understand this thing.*

spectacle *noun,* display, show. *The way he worked was an astonishing spectacle.*

② Read the Selection

1. Ask the students to listen to find out what happens when the bluejay finds the perfect place to store acorns. The first reading should be presented with minimal interruption. If a student does ask a question, answer it and continue reading.

2. After reading the selection, ask the students, Why was the bluejay so frustrated?

③ Present the Graphic Organizer

1. Display the graphic organizer, and point out that it can help us remember the main elements in the story.

2. Explain to the students that they will work through the organizer with you.

④ Use the Graphic Organizer

Reread the selection in sections, and ask questions that will help the students identify the primary elements in the story. Suggestions are with the selection. If necessary, model the thinking process.

Write the information on your organizer.

You may write words or sentences or draw quick sketches with labels.

Story Elements

This graphic organizer works well for identifying the elements of a short story and often the elements of a short nonfiction narrative.

Setting

| Time: (Answers may vary.) Sunday morning | Place: California |

Characters

Jim Baker, bluejays

Problem

The bluejay is mad because he can't fill up his hole with acorns.

Climax

After many bluejays examine the outside, an old jay goes inside and cracks the mystery.

Resolution

Bluejays laugh at their own foolishness.

Baker's Bluejay Yarn

from A Tramp Abroad
by Mark Twain

Animals talk to each other, of course. There can be no question about that; but I suppose there are very few people who can understand them. I never knew but one man who could. I knew he could, however, because he told me so himself. He was a middle-aged, simple-hearted miner who had lived in a lonely corner of California, among the woods and mountains, a good many years, and had studied the ways of his only neighbors, the beasts and the birds, until he believed he could accurately translate any remark which they made. This was Jim Baker. According to Jim Baker, some animals have only a limited education, and use only very simple words, and scarcely ever a comparison or a flowery figure; whereas, certain other animals have a large vocabulary, a fine command of language and a ready and fluent delivery; consequently these latter talk a great deal; they like it; they are conscious of their talent, and they enjoy "showing off." Baker said, that after long and careful observation, he had come to the conclusion that the bluejays were the best talkers he had found among birds and beasts. Said he:

"There's more *to* a bluejay than any other creature. He has got more moods, and more different kinds of feelings than other creatures; and, mind you, whatever a bluejay feels, he can put into language. And no mere commonplace language, either, but rattling, out-and-out book-talk—and bristling with metaphor, too—just bristling! And as for command of language—why *you* never see a bluejay get stuck for a word. No man ever did. They just boil out of him! And another thing: I've noticed a good deal, and there's no bird, or cow, or anything that uses as good grammar as a bluejay. You may say a cat uses good grammar. Well, a cat does—but you let a cat get excited once; you let a cat get to pulling fur with another cat on a shed, nights, and you'll hear grammar that will give you the lockjaw. Ignorant people think it's the *noise* which fighting cats make that is so aggravating, but it ain't so; it's the sickening grammar they use. Now I've never heard a jay use bad grammar but very seldom; and when they do, they are as ashamed as a human; they shut right down and leave.

This story is a tall tale. A tall tale is also called a "yarn." This type of story is very American—it has exaggeration and broad humor. Everything is bigger and better and faster and crazier than it really is. Tall tales are usually told in the language of the ordinary people. It's like the stories families pass on to each other.

We've met the main character of the story—a bluejay. Let's make a list of things we know about him so far.

"You may call a jay a bird. Well, so he is, in a measure—but he's got feathers on him, and don't belong to no church, perhaps; but otherwise he is just as much human as you be. And I'll tell you for why. A jay's gifts, and instincts, and feelings, and interests, cover the whole ground. A jay hasn't got any more principle than a Congressman. A jay will lie, a jay will steal, a jay will deceive, a jay will betray; and four times out of five, a jay will go back on his solemnest promise. The sacredness of an obligation is a thing which you can't cram into no bluejay's head. Now, on top of all this, there's another thing; a jay can out-swear any gentleman in the mines. You think a cat can swear. Well, a cat can; but you give a bluejay a subject that calls for his reserve-powers, and where is your cat? Don't talk to me—I know too much about this thing. And there's yet another thing; in the one little particular of scolding—just good, clean, out-and-out scolding—a bluejay can lay over anything, human or divine. Yes, sir, a jay is everything that a man is. A jay can cry, a jay can laugh, a jay can feel shame, a jay can reason and plan and discuss, a jay likes gossip and scandal, a jay has got a sense of humor, a jay knows when he is a donkey just as well as you do—maybe better. If a jay ain't human, he better take in his sign, that's all. Now I'm going to tell you a perfectly true fact about some bluejays.

We know the setting is out in the wilderness because Jim Baker tells us that he is the last one in the region. He lives in a cabin, and it's before California became a state.

"When I first begun to understand jay language correctly, there was a little incident happened here. Seven years ago, the last man in this region but me moved away. There stands his house—been empty ever since; a log house, with a plank roof—just one big room, and no more; no ceiling—nothing between the rafters and the floor. Well, one Sunday morning I was sitting out here in front of my cabin, with my cat, taking the sun, and looking at the blue hills, and listening to the leaves rustling so lonely in the trees, and thinking of the home away yonder in the states, that I hadn't heard from in thirteen years, when a bluejay lit on that house, with an acorn in his mouth, and says, 'Hello, I reckon I've struck something.' When he spoke, the acorn dropped out of his mouth and rolled down the roof, of course, but he didn't care; his mind was all on the thing he had struck. It was a knot-hole in the roof. He cocked his head to one side, shut one eye and put the other one to the hole, like a possum looking down a jug; then he glanced up with his bright eyes, gave a wink or two with his wings—which signifies gratification, you understand—and says, 'It looks like a hole, it's located like a hole—blamed if I don't believe it *is* a hole!'

We've been introduced to the bluejay's problem: Can he fill this perfectly elegant hole with acorns?

"Then he cocked his head down and took another look; he glances up perfectly joyful, this time; winks his wings and his tail both, and says, 'Oh, no, this ain't no fat thing, I reckon! If I ain't in luck! —why it's a perfectly elegant hole!' So he flew down and got that acorn, and fetched it up and dropped it in, and was just tilting his head back, with the heavenliest smile on his face, when all of a sudden he was paralyzed into a listening attitude and that smile faded gradually out of his countenance like breath off'n a razor, and the queerest look of surprise took its place. Then he says, 'Why, I didn't hear it fall!' He cocked his eye at the hole again, and took a long look; raised up and shook his head; stepped around to the other side of the hole and took another look from that side; shook his head again. He studied a while, then he just went into the details—walked round and round the hole and spied into it from every point of the compass. No use. Now he took a thinking attitude on the comb of the roof and scratched the back of his head with his right foot a minute, and finally says, 'Well, it's too many for *me,* that's certain; must be a mighty long hole; however, I ain't got no time to fool around here, I got to 'tend to business; I reckon it's all right— chance it, anyway.'

"So he flew off and fetched another acorn and dropped it in, and tried to flirt his eye to the hole quick enough to see what become of it, but he was too late. He held his eye there as much as a minute; then he raised up and sighed, and says, 'Confound it, I don't seem to understand this thing, no way; however, I'll tackle her again.' He fetched another acorn, and done his level best to see what become of it, but he couldn't. He says, 'Well, I never struck no such a hole as this before; I'm of the opinion it's a totally new kind of a hole.' Then he begun to get mad. He held in for a spell, walking up and down the comb of the roof and shaking his head and muttering to himself; but his feelings got the upper hand of him, presently, and he broke loose and cussed himself black in the face. I never see a bird take on so about a little thing. When he got through he walks to the hole and looks in again for half a minute; then he says, 'Well, you're a long hole, and a deep hole, and a mighty singular hole altogether—but I've started in to fill you, and I'm darned if I *don't* fill you, if it takes a hundred years!'

"And with that, away he went. You never see a bird work so since you was born. He laid into his work, and the way he hove acorns into that hole for about two hours and a half was one of the most exciting and astonishing spectacles I ever struck. He never stopped to take a look any more—he just hove 'em in and went for more. Well, at last he could hardly flop his wings, he was so tuckered out. He comes a-drooping down, once more, sweating like an ice-pitcher, drops his acorn in and says, '*Now* I guess I've got the bulge on you by this time!' So he bent down for a look. If you'll believe me, when his head come up again he was just pale with rage. He says, 'I've shoveled acorns enough in there to keep the family thirty years, and if I can see a sign of one of 'em I wish I may land in a museum with a belly full of sawdust in two minutes!'

"He just had strength enough to crawl up on to the comb and lean his back agin the chimbly, and then he collected his impressions and begun to free his mind. I see in a second that what I had mistook for profanity in the mines was only just the rudiments, as you may say.

"Another jay was going by, and heard him doing his devotions, and stops to inquire what was up. The sufferer told him the whole circumstance, and says, 'Now yonder's the hole, and if you don't believe me, go and look for yourself.' So this fellow went and looked, and comes back and says, 'How many did you say you put in there?' 'Not any less than two tons,' says the sufferer. The other jay went and looked again. He couldn't seem to make it out, so he raised a yell, and three more jays come. They all examined the hole, they all made the sufferer tell it over again, then they all discussed it, and got off as many leather-headed opinions about it as an average crowd of humans could have done.

We reached the highest point of the story, the climax. What was the solution to the bluejay's problem? Was he able to fill the hole with acorns? Why not?

"They called in more jays; then more and more, till pretty soon this whole region 'peared to have a blue flush about it. There must have been five thousand of them; and such another jawing and disputing and ripping and cussing, you never heard. Every jay in the whole lot put his eye to the hole and delivered a more chuckle-headed opinion about the mystery than the jay that went there before him. They examined the house all over, too. The door was standing half open, and at last one old jay happened to go and light on it and look in. Of course, that knocked the mystery galley-west in a second. There lay the acorns, scattered all over the floor. He flopped his wings and raised a whoop. 'Come here!' he says, 'Come here, everybody; hang'd if this fool hasn't been trying to fill up a house with acorns!' They all came a-swooping down like a blue cloud, and as each fellow lit on the door and took a glance, the whole absurdity of the contract that that first jay had tackled hit him home and he fell over backward suffocating with laughter, and the next jay took his place and done the same.

And how did the bluejays react to the situation? What do you think this story tells us about people?

"Well, sir, they roosted around here on the housetop and the trees for an hour, and guffawed over that thing like human beings. It ain't any use to tell me a bluejay hasn't got a sense of humor, because I know better. And memory, too. They brought jays here from all over the United States to look down that hole, every summer for three years. Other birds, too. And they could all see the point except an owl that come from Nova Scotia to visit the Yo Semite, and he took this thing in on his way back. He said he couldn't see anything funny in it. But then he was a good deal disappointed about Yo Semite, too."

5 Assess Understanding

1. Distribute copies of the graphic organizer.

2. Tell the students to listen to the selection again and make notes or draw pictures to help them remember what happened in the story.

3. Reread the selection.

Animals
Ecosystems: The Circle of Life

NON FICTION

LESSON MAP

1 Getting Started.

2 Read the selection to the group.

3 Present the graphic organizer.

4 Read the selection to the group while working with them to use the graphic organizer.

5 Assess understanding.

MATERIALS

Graphic Organizer #3—Chain of Events: displayed on an overhead; a copy for each student

Related Web sites: http://library.thinkquest.org/11353/ecosystems.htm
http://www.mbgnet.net/
http://www.windows.ucar.edu/tour/link=/earth/ecosystems.html&edu=elem
http://www.nhptv.org/natureworks/nwepecosystems.htm

1 Getting Started

BACKGROUND

1. An ecosystem is made up of climate and the animals and plants that live in that climate. Something as simple as climate temperature can affect which animals live in that environment, where they live, what they eat, and many other things. In this selection, find out how climate affects the circle of life.

VOCABULARY

Present the vocabulary words, using this format:

Succumb is a verb that means **to give in.** What is **succumb?** *Succumb is a verb that means to give in.*

Listen. **Mary succumbed to her hunger and ate a hamburger.** Say that. *Mary succumbed to her hunger and ate a hamburger.*

burrow *noun*, a hole. *Groundhogs dig burrows in the ground.*

nomad *noun*, a person who travels all the time. *The nomad needs to find new grass to feed his cows, so he travels all the time.*

camouflage *verb*, to blend into the color of the surroundings. *The lizard camouflages itself as the color of the tree.*

② Read the Selection

1. Ask the students to listen to find out how the chain of life works in ecosystems. The first reading should be presented with minimal interruption. If a student does ask a question, answer it and continue reading.

2. After reading the selection, ask the students, *What sorts of climate characteristics affect an animal's habitat, food, and survival techniques?*

③ Present the Graphic Organizer

1. Display the graphic organizer, and point out that constructing a chain of events can help us remember the main events in the story.

2. Explain to the students that they will work through the organizer with you.

④ Use the Graphic Organizer

Reread the selection in sections, and ask questions that will help the students identify the primary events in the story. Suggestions are with the selection. If necessary, model the thinking process.

Write the information on your organizer.

You may write words or sentences or draw quick sketches with labels.

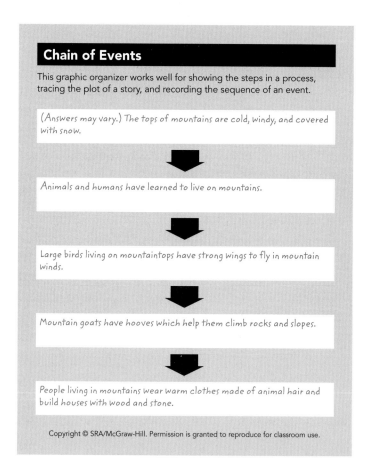

Chain of Events

This graphic organizer works well for showing the steps in a process, tracing the plot of a story, and recording the sequence of an event.

(Answers may vary.) The tops of mountains are cold, windy, and covered with snow.

⬇

Animals and humans have learned to live on mountains.

⬇

Large birds living on mountaintops have strong wings to fly in mountain winds.

⬇

Mountain goats have hooves which help them climb rocks and slopes.

⬇

People living in mountains wear warm clothes made of animal hair and build houses with wood and stone.

Ecosystems: The Circle of Life
by Louisa Webster

Mountains

Mountains are some of the most amazing places on Earth. Mountains have three parts: tops, slopes, and forests. The tops of mountains are cold, windy, or covered with snow. Steep, rocky hills called slopes are just below. Then thin forests begin. Many pine trees bloom in forests.

Both animals and humans have learned how to live on mountains. Large birds, like the golden eagle, live on mountaintops. Their strong wings help them fly in the mountain winds.

Mountain goats also live on mountaintops. They have hooves on their paws. Hooves help goats climb the rocks and steep slopes so they can get to and eat the grass on the cool mountainside.

Some mountain animals have thick hair to keep warm. The yak's long hair hangs loose near the ground.

Other animals, like the bear and the snow leopard, stay warm in dens or caves. Others, like the red deer, seek shelter under trees and shrubs.

People have found ways to live in the mountains. They wear warm clothes made from the hair of animals they've caught. Some people burn animal droppings to make fires. They build houses with stone and wood. They grow food crops on steps cut into the hillsides.

People have found ways to travel in the mountains too. Streets wind up and down the slopes. High bridges carry cars and trains across deep canyons. Tunnels lead through solid rock.

Both humans and wildlife have made the mountains their home.

Deserts

Twenty percent of Earth is desert. Deserts are very dry. Fewer than ten inches of rain fall each year. Plants, animals, and people have lived in deserts for a long time. They have many ways to survive in these dry places. They do not succumb to the dryness.

All plants, even desert plants, need water. Some store water in their leaves and stems. Others have deep roots that climb through the soil to find water. The roots of the saguaro cactus are shallow. They spread far and wide and find water.

Rabbits and lizards keep their limbs cool in tunnels underground. Goats stay in the shade under cliffs. A camel can go days without food or water, because its hump stores fat, which gives it energy. Two sets of eyelashes keep out the sun and the sand.

An ecosystem is first and foremost decided by the climate, whether that climate is a cold and windy mountaintop or the hot desert. The climate affects the types of shelter that are available, as well as food and water. How does the hot sun affect plants and animals?

People have found many ways to live in the desert without succumbing to the weather. Pipes and canals carry caught water from rivers to desert cities. The pipes also carry water to crops in farm fields. Deep wells and juicy plants have water that people can use.

Some people use layers of cloth to keep themselves safe. Cloth covers their heads and limbs from the sun. It also blocks the blowing sand.

Life on the desert continues. Plants, animals, and people have found ways to survive there.

Plains

Most plains are lands that are flat, are covered in grass, and have very few trees. Plains cover about 25 percent of Earth's land. Rainfall on the plains is between 10 and 40 inches a year. There is little or no shade. The grasses grow well because of the rich soil and strong sunlight.

The plains are full of life. Grass and seeds feed lots of insects. Butterflies and grasshoppers fly around in the air. Termites and ants climb beneath the soil. Birds and other animals feast on the seeds and the insects they have caught.

Animals have found ways to live well on the plains. Prairie dogs dig burrows in the dirt. Zebras bite off the grasses with their sharp front teeth. They grind grass with their wide back teeth. Anteaters use their long snouts to search and comb through tunnels for bugs.

Hawks and eagles spot prey from the sky. Antelopes' long legs help them escape the cheetah.

Some people live on the plains as nomads. They live in tents. Their cows need fresh grass to survive, so the nomads move from place to place.

The first people to live on plains built houses out of thick pieces of dirt and grass. In the rich soil, they grew corn and wheat for food.

Today, too much farming is hurting the plains. Because of this farming, something must be done to keep the plains healthy.

Forests and Rain Forests

Many forms of life live in forests and rain forests. From the ground to the treetops, there is a lot going on.

Forest animals know how to live in a warm or cold climate. Rain forest creatures live all year in a hot, steamy place.

The plains have lots of grass with few trees and lots of rain. How does this climate affect where animals and people live? How have plants adapted to the climate?

In forests and rain forests, plants and animals know how to survive. In winter, forest creatures stay warm in dens. Some eat nuts and berries. In the rain forest, plants have thick, waxy leaves. Plants can control water better with waxy leaves.

Forest creatures know ways to stay safe. Porcupines and monkeys climb trees. Bats and birds fly. Tree frogs grip branches with their feet. Insects camouflage themselves. This means they are the same color as leaves, twigs, and bark, so other animals can't see them.

Forest critters have many ways of getting food. The owl's eyes help it look for mice at night. The spider builds webs to catch insects. The orangutan follows birds that like the same food it likes. The sloth bear kneels down and uses its long tongue to slurp up termites.

People know ways to live in the forest too. Some people build fires to cook their food, and some make their clothes and tools and build houses from forest things.

In Cambodia, some cities are very near rain forests. In strong rains, Cambodia's lakes get bigger. Some people live on the lakes!

Oceans

The ocean covers 71 percent of our planet. The ocean is home to many kinds of sea life. Each animal and plant has a special body. Some animals even have special senses. These things help them look for food and find ways to survive in deep, dark waters.

Many sea animals must swim to look for food. Some use their fins and tails to push themselves forward through the water. The smooth bodies of stingrays and sharks help them glide. Squids and clams know to move by shooting jets of water from their bodies.

How do lionfish protect themselves from predators in the ocean?

Sea animals know many ways to stay safe in the ocean. Lots of small fish move together in a group. This is a school of fish. Oysters have hard shells. Lionfish have sharp spines like little hooks. Some sea animals hide from their enemies by using camouflage.

Just like animals on land, sea animals need oxygen. Oxygen is in the air and the water. Some sea animals absorb oxygen through their skin. Some use their gills to breathe. Others, like whales and seals, go to the surface to breathe air.

People have also learned to live by the ocean. They catch many kinds of fish with large nets. Then they eat the fish, or they sell the fish and make money. People also catch, sell, and cook shrimps, lobsters, and crabs.

Many ocean creatures have found ways to survive.

⑤ Assess Understanding

1. Distribute copies of the graphic organizer.

2. Tell the students to listen to the selection again and make notes or draw pictures to help them remember what happened in the story.

3. Reread the selection.

Lesson 3

Animals

Three Men and a Horse

NON FICTION

LESSON MAP

1 Getting Started.

2 Read the selection to the group.

3 Present the graphic organizer.

4 Read the selection to the group while working with them to use the graphic organizer.

5 Assess understanding.

MATERIALS

● Graphic Organizer #4—Facts and Feelings/Opinions: displayed on an overhead; a copy for each student

● Related Web sites: http://www.littletongov.org/history/biographies/moody.asp
http://www.pbs.org/wgbh/amex/seabiscuit/
http://www.racingmuseum.org/hall/horse.asp?ID=132
http://news.nationalgeographic.com/news/2003/07/0728_030728_seabiscuit.html

1 Getting Started

BACKGROUND

1. Ralph Moody was best known for his "Little Britches" series of books that are loosely based on actual people and fictional characters.

VOCABULARY

Present the vocabulary words, using this format:

Two lunger is a noun that means **a two-cycle internal combustion engine.** What is **two lunger?** *Two lunger is a noun that means a two-cycle internal combustion engine.*

Listen. **Most of the early automobiles in San Francisco were "two lunger" Buicks.** Say that. *Most of the early automobiles in San Francisco were "two lunger" Buicks.*

prominent *adjective,* famous, important. *Charles Howard was prominent in California horse circles.*

school of hard knocks *idiom,* on the streets, life experiences. *He learned his trade in the school of hard knocks.*

horsebreaker *noun,* horse trainer. *Tom was hired as a horsebreaker, often riding thirty bucking horses a day.*

Thoroughbred *noun,* a breed of race horses. *Tom was forty-three years old before he had a chance to train a Thoroughbred.*

companionship *noun,* friendship. *Part of Seabiscuit's temper was cured by his companionship with Pumpkin.*

2 Read the Selection

1. Ask the students to listen to find out about the three men who helped make Seabiscuit a champion race horse. The first reading should be presented with minimal interruption. If a student does ask a question, answer it and continue reading.

2. After reading the selection, ask the students, Which of these men do you think was most responsible for making Seabiscuit a champion?

3 Present the Graphic Organizer

1. Display the graphic organizer, and clarify differences between facts and opinions.

2. Explain to the students that they will work through the organizer with you.

4 Use the Graphic Organizer

Reread the selection in sections, and ask questions that will help the students identify facts and opinions. Suggestions are with the selection. If necessary, model the thinking process.

Write the information on your organizer.

You may write words or sentences or draw quick sketches with labels.

Facts and Feelings/Opinions

This graphic organizer works well for distinguishing between facts and opinions.

Facts:
1. (Answers may vary.) Charles Howard bought Seabiscuit.
2. When Tom Smith was 6, his family moved to Texas.
3. When he was 13, Smith worked with a professional horsebreaker.
4. Howard took Smith to look for horses in the East.
5. Smith told Howard to buy Seabiscuit.

Feelings/Opinions:
1. Howard must be out of his mind to buy Seabiscuit.
2. Howard was a keen businessman.
3. He's a bad actor.
4. He is one of the best horses in the business.
5. Red Pollard was one of the better jockeys.

Three Men and a Horse

from Come On, Seabiscuit
by Ralph Moody

This paragraph is full of opinions. Even when a fact is stated it's connected to opinions. I'll read the sentences one at a time, and you tell me whether the statement is a fact or an opinion.

The railbirds nearly split their sides with laughing when the news was circulated that Charles Howard had bought Seabiscuit, and that old Tom Smith had said he could improve the colt. Nothing could have seemed more ridiculous. Who was this man Howard, and what did he know about race horses? He must be out of his mind if he thought an old-time cowboy could improve a horse that had been trained by Sunny Jim Fitzsimmons—the man who had developed two of the only three horses in history ever to win the Triple Crown. Poor Seabiscuit! He was on the skids for sure, but what difference? Those weak knees of his wouldn't hold up for more than another race or two anyway. If they would, smart old Sunny Jim would never have let the colt go. The railbirds would have laughed still louder if they had known who Seabiscuit's jockey would be.

As a young man Charles Howard had opened a little bicycle repair shop in San Francisco. That was before there were any garages, so the few people who owned automobiles took them to the bicycle shop when they needed repairing. Most of the very early automobiles in San Francisco were "two lunger" Buicks, so it was only natural that young Howard should become the Buick agent in the city.

How were Charles Howard's opinions different from the Buick company's opinions?

When, after the great San Francisco earthquake and fire, automobiles began replacing carriage horses, Charles Howard's business began to boom. He was selling Buicks faster than he could get them shipped from Detroit to the West Coast. When he doubled his orders, the company cautioned him that he might find himself overstocked, since most people still preferred the driving horse to the automobile.

Young as he was, Charles Howard was already a keen, farsighted businessman. He wrote back, "I must have the cars I have ordered as fast as you can get them here. The day of the horse is past, and the people in San Francisco want automobiles. I wouldn't give five dollars for the best horse in this country."

Wrong as he later proved himself to be about what he would pay for the best horse in the country, his foresight regarding automobiles was keen and accurate. Because of it, he became a multimillionaire, and the biggest automobile distributor on the West Coast. He bought a beautiful ranch in the redwood country of northern California, stocked it with excellent ponies when his sons proved to be fine polo players, and became prominent in California horse circles.

Late in 1933 pari-mutuel wagering on horse races was legalized in California, and as a result, several of the finest racing establishments in the world were built in the state. The cost of building a racing plant is enormous, and the money is usually furnished by very wealthy men who have a love for horses. Charles Howard had both the love for horses and the wealth, so was one of the Californians to finance the famous Santa Anita track. With his large investment in a race track, it was only natural that he should become interested in Thoroughbred race horses, and should decide to establish a racing stable. But he knew very little about Thoroughbreds, and there were no famous trainers in California, such as Sunny Jim Fitzsimmons. Tom Smith, the man Mr. Howard chose as his advisor and trainer, was about the most unlikely one imaginable.

"Silent Tom" Smith was fifty-seven years old when a friend sent him to Charles Howard to ask for a job as a horse trainer. He was a quiet, dead-broke, little man, and his only education had been received in the school of hard knocks. When he was six, his family had moved from Georgia to Texas, and he had grown up in a saddle. Then, when he was thirteen, he had worked with a professional horsebreaker. Learning to ride wild broncos could hardly be expected to fit a boy to become a trainer of Thoroughbred horses, but Tom Smith not only learned to ride outlaw horses, he learned to understand them—and he never stopped learning.

Listen carefully to the following description of Tom Smith and try to find two facts and two opinions that show us that Tom was a good horse trainer.

By the time Tom became twenty-one he was a top-notch cowboy, and had gained a reputation that was rare, even in Texas. It was claimed that he could keep the upper hand with any animal, and that no horse had ever been known to get the better of him. Because he preferred to work alone and had little to say when with other men, he was given the name of Silent Tom, and it was believed that he had a secret about controlling animals which he wouldn't tell. He did have a secret, and he wouldn't tell it for fear he might be ridiculed. From the time he was a boy, he had believed that animals reacted the same as people did, that whenever one became an outlaw or misbehaved there was a cause for it, and that the fault could be corrected if the cause were discovered. The reason for his preferring to work alone was that he could study the causes better in that way. And the reason for his silence was that the communication between men and animals must be through understanding, not conversation.

With the outbreak of the Boer War in 1899, the British government sent agents to the United States to buy fifty thousand cavalry horses. There was only one place where any such number of horses suitable for cavalry use could be found: in the wild mustang herds that roamed the prairies of Texas, Colorado, Wyoming, and Montana. The Moncrief brothers went into the business of catching and breaking these wild horses, offering to pay seventy-five dollars a month for cowboys who would tackle the rough and dangerous job. That was more than twice what Tom Smith was making as a cowhand, and exactly the kind of job he liked, so he hired out to the Moncriefs as a horsebreaker. Until the order was filled, he often rode as many as thirty bucking horses in a single day—and from every one of them he learned to understand horses a little better.

After working for the Moncriefs Tom didn't return to Texas, but took a job as foreman on the Unaweep Cattle Range at Grand Junction, Colorado. In those days the foreman on a big cattle ranch had to be veterinarian, horse trainer, and often blacksmith, as well as bossing the cowhands and planning the roundups. Tom Smith went at his foreman's job in the same way he had gone at horsebreaking—

by studying it out instead of guessing, and by listening instead of talking. In Grand Junction there was a livery stable owner named Guy Bedwell, who was a great talker, and who later became the greatest Thoroughbred trainer of his time. Like all great talkers, the people he liked best were those who were good listeners, and "Silent Tom" Smith was one of the best.

Whenever the crew from the Unaweep Range rode into town for a Saturday night blowout, Tom spent his time at Bedwell's livery stable, listening and learning. And in appreciation, Guy Bedwell taught him many of the tricks of the training art: how to shoe a horse so as to correct the faults in its gait; how to build its running muscles, fire a bowed tendon, bandage and treat a sprained joint, mix his own liniments and medicines, balance a diet, and a hundred other little tricks that are known only by an expert trainer.

The close friendship between Tom and Guy continued until 1906, when Bedwell sold his livery stable and went on to become the most renowned Thoroughbred trainer of that period. For another fifteen years Tom stayed on the Unaweep Range as foreman, but he never forgot a lesson he had learned from his friend Bedwell, and he never forgot his yearning to become a trainer of Thoroughbreds himself.

Tom Smith was forty-three years old before he had his first chance to try his hand as a trainer of Thoroughbreds—and it wasn't much of a chance. In 1921 the owners of the ranch sold out, and Tom found a job as foreman with McCarty and Landrum. Their business was that of furnishing bucking broncos for small rodeos throughout the West. They also had a half dozen Thoroughbreds that they shipped along with the broncos, for putting on relay races. Every one of them was an abused and broken-down old race horse, worth less than a hundred dollars. One or two were seemingly hopeless outlaws, and all the others had sprained knees, cracked hoofs, bowed tendons, or broken wind. But they were Thoroughbreds, the horses Tom Smith had yearned to handle and train for more than twenty years, and he went to work on them as carefully as though each one had been a Triple Crown winner.

Through understanding, patience, and patchwork, Tom improved his half dozen old has-beens until they were winning far more than their share of the races at the little bush-circuit rodeos. His success with them brought him to the attention of "Cowboy Charlie" Irwin, of the Irwin Livestock and Show Company. Cowboy Charlie was then promoting and furnishing horses—both bucking and racing—for frontier shows in every part of the West, from the Missouri River to the Pacific Coast, and from Canada to Mexico. His horses were of about the same quality as those owned by McCarty and Landrum, but he was a big operator, and had many more of them—sometimes as many as fifty racers. What he needed badly was a man who could keep them patched up enough to race after taking the punishment of being shipped from town to town in boxcars, and Tom Smith proved to be exactly the right man.

For more than ten years Tom worked as foreman for Cowboy Charlie Irwin, constantly on the move from one frontier show to another, and constantly patching up the broken-down old nags that were put into his care. It isn't at all strange that, with so much practice, he became the best horse patcher in the business. But Tom Smith was never satisfied with doing only a patchwork job. He studied every Thoroughbred turned over to him as carefully as though it had been worth a thousand times its cost. His first care was to gain an understanding between himself and the horse. Then he set about healing its injuries as much as they could be healed, correcting its faults when they could be corrected, strengthening its body through proper feeding and training, and rekindling its determination to win.

During the World's Fair at Chicago, Tom reached the top as a bush-league horse trainer. At that time a nine-day rodeo was held at Soldiers Field, just outside the Fair Grounds, and Tom's patched-up old racers won sixteen of the eighteen racing events. Then Cowboy Charlie Irwin was killed in an automobile accident—and Tom Smith was out of a job. Pari-mutuel wagering on horse races had just been legalized in California, and racing was becoming a popular sport, so Tom went there to look for a job. He had been there only a short time when a friend told him, "Charlie Howard, the wealthy Buick man, bought seventeen Thoroughbred yearlings at Saratoga lately, and he needs a trainer for them. Why don't you go and see if you can get the job?"

Why do you think Tom wanted Mr. Howard to buy Seabiscuit? List at least two facts to support your opinion.

Tom got the job of training the yearlings—and more. He won the complete confidence and trust of his new boss. Mr. Howard took him East to see what they could pick up in the way of a few inexpensive Thoroughbreds; horses that could be raced on the new California tracks until the yearlings would be ready in a year or two. They had looked at scores of Thoroughbreds before Tom saw Seabiscuit run in the Mohawk Claiming Stakes, recognized his quality, courage, and determination at a glance, and told his boss, "Get me that horse. I can improve him."

Mr. Howard was going to Detroit from New York, so Seabiscuit was taken along in order that Tom might study him, and if he thought best, try him out in a race or two there. It didn't require much study for Tom to find out that the colt was extremely intelligent, and that his misbehavior was due to pain, frustration, and exhaustion. He had long ago discovered that highly intelligent horses reacted exactly the same as highly intelligent people. When overworked, in pain, frustrated, and physically exhausted, they lost their appetites, and their nervous systems became upset, making them irritable and resentful of any attempt to force them.

Seabiscuit's lack of appetite and continual walking in his stall were positive proof that his nerves were on edge. He laid his ears back, snapped, and threatened to attack whenever a groom went into his stall. He hung back and sulked when taken out for his morning exercise, was unruly at the starting gate, and fought against any restraint or urging when on the track. Tom set about to correct these bad habits by removing the cause, rather than by the use of force.

Tom had decided to make the colt's first workout a slow canter, just enough to give him a little exercise. But Seabiscuit decided to show his resentment of restraint by making it into a runaway. Tom let him run—for a full two miles. There isn't much fun in fighting against a man who won't fight back, and there isn't much chance to show resentment against restraint when there isn't any. After his two-mile runaway, Seabiscuit came to the conclusion that it was senseless and a waste of energy to fight against his new trainer. He behaved himself on the way back to the barn, and by the time he had been cooled out he was hungry enough that he was glad to take a carrot from Tom's hand.

When a person who is nervous and upset is left alone, he will brood about his troubles, and the more he broods the more irritable and disagreeable he will become. But if he has company, he is less inclined to think about himself and the injustices that have been done him. Then too, even though we don't particularly want something that we have, we dislike having someone else try to take it away from us. In boyhood, Tom Smith had noticed that animals had these same traits, so he tried an experiment on Seabiscuit. He put a nanny goat in the stall with him. Just having company was enough to stop the nervous colt from his continual stall walking. The goat was a curiosity to him, and except for its greediness, they might have become good friends.

Although Seabiscuit had been a heavy feeder before he was put into racing, his appetite had decreased as the strain on his nerves and the pain of his injured knee had increased. He had become a nibbler and a picker, but there was nothing the matter with Nanny's appetite. At feeding time she climbed right atop the forkful of hay, trying to stow it all away before Seabiscuit could get any. Even though he wasn't hungry, he had no intention of letting her hog the whole meal, so for a couple of feedings he tried to get his share. But Nanny was just too greedy to be put up with. When she climbed onto the next forkful, Seabiscuit picked her up by the scruff of the neck. Holding her firmly in his teeth, he walked once around the stall, giving her a good shaking, then set her down outside the doorway where a groom could rescue her.

Though Tom's goat experiment hadn't been entirely successful, it had done the two things he was most anxious for. It had shown that with a companion in the stall Seabiscuit's nerves would quiet enough to keep him from his continual walking, and that, with a little competition, his appetite could be stimulated. The next task was to find him the best possible stall companion, and Tom didn't have much trouble in doing it.

At all race tracks there are ponies which are used for leading fractious Thoroughbreds to the starting gate. They are usually little fellows, not worth very much, and their greatest requirement is that they be gentle and friendly, so as to quiet the horse that is being led. At the Fair Grounds track in Detroit there was a little palomino lead pony, named Pumpkin because of his golden color. He was nine years old, and not much of a horse, but he was gentle and friendly with other horses, so when Seabiscuit tossed the goat out, Tom Smith put Pumpkin into a double stall with him. Within an hour he and Seabiscuit had formed a friendship that lasted the rest of their lives, and the war of nerves was nearly won. Seabiscuit quit his habit of stall walking entirely, his appetite became much better, and with it his disposition improved remarkably. He seemed to sense that he was no longer an outcast, but among friends, and his resentment of handling was rapidly forgotten.

Whatever part of Seabiscuit's irritability wasn't cured by understanding treatment, and his companionship with Pumpkin, was taken care of by Silent Tom's skill as a veterinarian and his years of experience in patching up broken-down race horses. He devised braces for the colt's sprained ankle and knee; flexible enough that he could walk with them on, but strong enough to take the strain off as he stood in his stall, so as to relieve him of the constant, irritating pain. Since both knees and ankles had been weakened by overwork as a two-year-old, Tom rubbed them with a soothing liniment after every workout, put braces on them, padded them heavily with cotton, and bandaged all four legs from below the ankles to above the knees and hocks. One sport writer said in his column that "Smith's bandages look like World War One puttees," but they did the trick, strengthened the weakened joints, and worked wonders on Seabiscuit's disposition.

While Tom Smith was in Detroit, getting acquainted with Seabiscuit and discovering ways to correct his bad habits, two other down-and-out horsemen were making their way there for the races at the Fair Grounds, but their luck seemed to have run out. One of them was Jim Allen, known around the race tracks as Yummy. He was a jockey's agent but most of the boys he represented were small-time riders, there was a depression on, and Yummy had been barely making a living. He was driving one of his riders to Detroit in hope of finding him a few mounts to ride in the races, when his auto was wrecked in a collision. Both boys were badly shaken up, but they managed to hitch-hike their way to the city. They reached the Fair Grounds a couple of days after Tom Smith got there with Seabiscuit, and between them they had $7.60 and two soiled shirts.

What are two things you found out about Red Pollard?

The jockey that Yummy brought to Detroit was Jack Pollard, known at the small-time race tracks of the West as "Red," and in the smaller-time boxing rings at the Frontier shows and carnivals as "The Cougar." Red Pollard was born in Alberta, Canada, in 1909. Ever since he became seventeen he had been kicking around the West—riding any race horse he could get to ride, and boxing any bantam-weight who dared to get into a ring with him. His love for Thoroughbreds was as deep as Tom Smith's, but the ones he'd had a chance to ride were mostly the same type as those Tom had been training. Although Red was one of the better jockeys on the bush circuit, he had won only three stake races in his life.

When the boys reached the Fair Grounds, Yummy took Red from trainer to trainer, trying to find him a horse to ride. He'd take anything, even an outlaw, just to earn a few dollars for room rent and grub. There were more jockeys than jobs, and every horse in every race was spoken for. Yummy had been to every trainer he knew, and to nearly every barn on the Fair Grounds, when a groom told him, "There's a new trainer here; one nobody never heard of before—a guy that won't do no talking. He fetched a gimpy colt out here from Saratoga a couple of days ago. I hear tell it belongs to some automobile man from out to California. Don't know if they're going to try racing the colt—he's a bad actor—but they've got him over in the east barn. Why don't you go see the guy? His name's Smith. You might pick the kid up a job as exercise boy."

It was late afternoon when Yummy and Red found the barn where Seabiscuit was stabled. Tom had bandaged the colt's legs for the night, and, as was his custom when getting acquainted with a new horse, was sitting just outside the stall doorway. He still had a lot of thinking and planning to do, and as he did it he was enjoying the afternoon sunshine—his camp chair leaned back against the barn, his battered old hat pulled down over his forehead, dark glasses protecting his eyes, and chewing the end of a straw. He was so busy with his thought that he didn't notice the two boys coming toward him until Yummy called out, "Good afternoon, Mr. Smith. I hear you've got a horse you might be needing a good jockey for. I've got one of the best in the business here. I want you to meet . . ."

Tom took the straw out of his mouth, grinned, and cut in, "You don't have to introduce me to The Cougar. We knowed each other on the leaky-roof circuit, when times was real tough."

"They're still tough," Red told him.

Tom Smith paid no more attention to Yummy, but told Red, "I've got a horse here named Seabiscuit. A better one than anybody thinks. I need a strong boy to handle him—one that's kicked around like you and me, and knows how to get along with the stove-up ones. You take a look at him, work him a little and we'll see."

It is well known that some men are exceptionally keen in their judgment of a horse. It is not so well known that exceptionally intelligent horses are equally good judges of men. They can tell from a man's scent whether he is afraid or assured, nervous or calm, rough or gentle, and above all, whether or not he is worthy of their trust and confidence.

Seabiscuit and Pumpkin were munching hay at the far side of the box stall when Red Pollard went to the doorway and leaned on the closed half-door. Pumpkin paid no attention, but Seabiscuit raised his head, turned it toward the doorway, and sniffed. For a minute he stood, sampling the scent of the boy whose head and shoulders showed above the half-door. What he read in that scent seemed to satisfy him. He left his hay, and came over to rub his muzzle against Red's shoulder.

What was Seabiscuit's opinion of Red? What facts tell us that?

There was no need for Charles Howard or Tom Smith to make any decision as to who their jockey would be; Seabiscuit had made the decision for himself. He stood, still rubbing his muzzle on the shoulder, while Red Pollard stroked his neck and told him, "We're goin' places together, Baby, you and me. There ain't nobody goin' to stop us—not nobody."

It was just soft-talk—the kind a man will talk to a horse he has fallen in love with—but Red believed it, and though Seabiscuit couldn't understand the words, he seemed to believe it too. When Tom Smith came to join them, the colt stood nuzzling them both. He had found the two men he trusted, the two men he wanted to please, and from that day he gave them the best he had. And they gave him all he had ever needed: understanding, painstaking care, and affection.

⑤ Assess Understanding

1. Distribute copies of the graphic organizer.

2. Tell the students to listen to the selection again and make notes or draw pictures to help them remember facts and opinions.

3. Reread the selection.

Animals

Swimming with Sharks

NON FICTION

LESSON MAP

1. Getting Started.

2. Read the selection to the group.

3. Present the graphic organizer.

4. Read the selection to the group while working with them to use the graphic organizer.

5. Assess understanding.

MATERIALS

- Graphic Organizer #6—Cluster Diagram: displayed on an overhead; a copy for each student

- Related Web sites: http://www.npr.org/templates/story/story.php?storyId=5037886
http://www.nationalgeographic.com/adventure/0511/whats_new/fabien_cousteau.html
http://www.pbs.org/wgbh/nova/sharks/
http://www.nationalgeographic.com/kids/creature_feature/0206/sharks.html

1 Getting Started

BACKGROUND

1. Fabien Cousteau is the grandson of Jacques-Yves Cousteau and the son of Jean-Michel Cousteau. All three have been extremely active in exploring and saving the ocean environments. Fabien's special interest is great white sharks.

VOCABULARY

Present the vocabulary words, using this format:

Rebreather is a noun that means a system that allows divers to rebreathe their air. What is **rebreather?** *Rebreather is a noun that means a system that allows divers to rebreathe their air.*

Listen. **Many divers use rebreathers instead of scuba gear.** Say that. *Many divers use rebreathers instead of scuba gear.*

feasible *adjective*, possible, practical. *It wasn't feasible to work from a rigid submarine.*

submersible *adjective*, underwater craft. *Submarines are submersible.*

infringe *verb*, violate, harm. *One way would be to infringe on another one's territory.*

terminating *verb*, ending. *(See example sentence below.)*

longevity, *noun*, long life. *Killing a juvenile female of the same species is basically terminating your longevity as a species.*

2 Read the Selection

1. Ask the students to listen to find out about the shark Cousteau's team built. The first reading should be presented with minimal interruption. If a student does ask a question, answer it and continue reading.

2. After reading the selection, ask the students, Would you like to explore the ocean in Cousteau's shark?

3 Present the Graphic Organizer

1. Display the graphic organizer, and discuss it briefly. Point out that this is a good way to show how pieces of information about one topic are related.

2. Explain to the students that they will work through the organizer with you.

4 Use the Graphic Organizer

Reread the selection in sections, and ask questions that will help the students identify how the shark was created. Suggestions are with the selection. If necessary, model the thinking process.

Write the information on your organizer.

You may write words or sentences or draw quick sketches with labels.

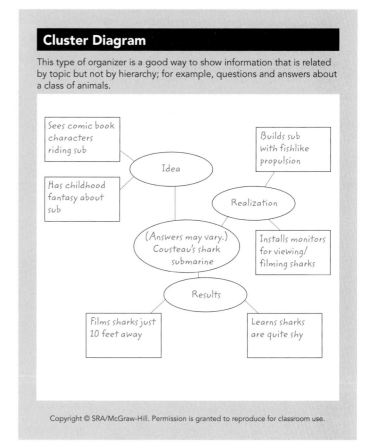

Cluster Diagram

This type of organizer is a good way to show information that is related by topic but not by hierarchy; for example, questions and answers about a class of animals.

Sees comic book characters riding sub

Builds sub with fishlike propulsion

Idea

Has childhood fantasy about sub

Realization

(Answers may vary.) Cousteau's shark submarine

Installs monitors for viewing/ filming sharks

Results

Films sharks just 10 feet away

Learns sharks are quite shy

Swimming with Sharks

from December 3, 2005, National Public Radio Interview

Think about the big subject of this interview. It tells about creating a shark-type submarine. So let's begin by writing "Shark Submarine" in the center of our diagram.

DEBBIE ELLIOTT, host: From three men in a tub to one man in a sub shaped like a great white shark. Remember the Greek soldiers hiding in a hollow wooden horse to fool their enemies during the Trojan War? Well, now the team of underwater explorer Fabien Cousteau, grandson of Jacques, has invented another decoy: a shark submarine aptly named Troy. Concealed in Troy, Fabien Cousteau spent hundreds of hours swimming with and filming great whites for an upcoming documentary called "Mind of a Demon." He joins us now from our New York bureau.

Welcome.

Mr. FABIEN COUSTEAU: Hello. Thank you very much.

ELLIOTT: You tagged along with your grandfather and father on many undersea adventures. Where did the idea for actually making your submarine shaped like a shark come from?

Where did Fabien get his idea for a shark submarine? I'll write that information in one of the little clusters.

Mr. COUSTEAU: Childhood fantasy. I'd grown up in both France and the United States. And in Europe there's a comic book called "TinTin" or "Tin-Tun." And one of the episodes is "Le trésor de Rackham le Rouge" or, in English, "Red Rackham's Treasure," in which—on the front cover as a matter of fact—there's a shark-shaped submersible where TinTin and his dog are in. And I thought that was a fantastic idea back when I was seven, eight years old, and I'd remembered that from back then, and I actually dug up the comic book. And that's what spurred it on.

ELLIOTT: Was it difficult trying to create a Trojan horse for the ocean?

Mr. COUSTEAU: Extremely. I also wanted it to be as realistic as possible. So as far as it being a rigid sub, it just didn't make that feasible. So we went to a wet submersible, which gave us the possibility of articulation, or in this case, fishlike propulsion, meaning that the shark submersible moves forward in a fishlike fashion by beating its tail.

ELLIOTT: Now when you say wet submersible, this means that unlike a submarine that we think of, say, in the Navy or something where people are walking around in a dry environment, you're actually in water inside of this shark vehicle?

Mr. COUSTEAU: Correct. I'm lying on my stomach basically and propped up on my elbows. I have about 80 pounds of rebreather on my back.

ELLIOTT: How do you see out? Are you looking out the eyes or the mouth or something?

What have we found out about the submarine or submersible? Let's add this to our cluster. I'll write *submarine* in an oval and the facts in the boxes.

Mr. COUSTEAU: I'm actually looking through two two-and-a-half-inch monitors that are in front of me, which also serve as the monitors to the cameras that are recording.

ELLIOTT: Do you think the sharks were actually fooled into thinking that you were one of them?

Mr. COUSTEAU: I can only hope. The signs point to yes, enough that they seemed to act very similarly to Troy as when they do amongst themselves, and that's in a very cautious way. I actually had a very hard time swimming up close enough to these animals to film them, and the reason for that is, basically, they don't take unnecessary risks. And one of them would be to infringe on another one's territory. Now that said, we were able to get some footage of a juvenile white shark, a female white shark, about nine feet long, that did violate that protocol and was going into the territorial area of a 14- or 15-foot female adult. Well, the female adult then chased the juvenile off by tagging her in the gill section with the gaping mouth and pushed her away that way, but never bit down. And that was fascinating. Just in that five seconds of footage it tells you a lot about this animal that thinks beyond just this mindless killing machine. It realizes that killing a juvenile female of the same species is basically terminating your longevity as a species.

ELLIOTT: How close did they come to you?

Was the experiment successful? I'll write *results* in an oval and the facts in the boxes.

Mr. COUSTEAU: When Troy was moving I got within, oh, about 20, 30 feet at best. When I decided to stop moving and just hover there for a bit, the animals would come in a little bit closer and get more curious. They wouldn't come in aggressively. They would come in a very shy, uh, curious fashion. So, you know, there were times where they got relatively close, probably 10, 15 feet away.

My hope was that Troy would be sexy enough that maybe an adult male might find some sort of a liking to her, and we did not go quite that far.

ELLIOTT: So you think people are misinformed about sharks, that they're afraid of sharks and think, in particular, the great white is this evil creature? Did you see or learn anything in your visits with these sharks that can help change that mind-set?

Mr. COUSTEAU: I think so. Up to now, the way you bring sharks–or white sharks–in is typically you throw in some chum or some tuna or whatever, and these animals have the singular notion that they're coming in to feed. Well, that's fine. But that said, we have footage in the documentary that shows how relatively placid they are, how relatively shy they are, and how different they are from the animals that are portrayed in your day-to-day, big-screen fiction movies. And although I'm all for fiction, we have to realize that that's exactly what it is.

ELLIOTT: Fabien Cousteau's upcoming CBS documentary is "Mind of a Demon." Thank you so much for joining us.

Mr. COUSTEAU: Thank you for having me.

5 Assess Understanding

1. Distribute copies of the graphic organizer.

2. Tell the students to listen to the selection again and make notes to help them remember information about the story.

3. Reread the selection.

Animals

A Safe Haven

NON FICTION

LESSON MAP

1 Getting Started.

2 Read the selection to the group.

3 Present the graphic organizer.

4 Read the selection to the group while working with them to use the graphic organizer.

5 Assess understanding.

MATERIALS

- Graphic Organizer #3—Chain of Events: displayed on an overhead; a copy for each student

- Related Web sites: http://www.bronxzoo.com/
http://www.reptilediscovery.com/retic.html
http://www.sandiegozoo.org/animalbytes/t-python.html

1 Getting Started

BACKGROUND

1. Pythons belong to the family of constrictor snakes. These snakes grab prey with their mouth, wrap their body around the victim, and suffocate it. They don't crush the prey—at least, not purposefully. Then the python swallows the prey whole. The reticulated python is the largest python, and it can grow to over 30 feet.

VOCABULARY

Present the vocabulary words, using this format:

Reticulated is an adjective that means **a pattern that looks like a network.** What is **reticulated?** *Reticulated is an adjective that means a pattern that looks like a network.*

Listen. **The reticulated python has a network-like pattern on its skin.** Say that. *The reticulated python has a network-like pattern on its skin.*

converted *verb*, changed into something else. *The snakes' skin could be converted into shoes, belts, and purses.*

ascend *verb*, move up. *Pythons often ascend trees to avoid capture.*

constrict *verb*, squeeze. *The python will constrict its prey to kill it.*

② Read the Selection

1. Ask the students to listen to find out about how Samantha got to the Bronx Zoo. The first reading should be presented with minimal interruption. If a student does ask a question, answer it and continue reading.

2. After reading the selection, ask the students, What did you find out about Samantha?

③ Present the Graphic Organizer

1. Display the graphic organizer, and discuss it briefly. Point out that this is a good way to track a series of events, the plot of a story, or steps in a process.

2. Explain to the students that they will work through the organizer with you.

④ Use the Graphic Organizer

Reread the selection in sections, and ask questions that will help the students identify the sequence of events. Suggestions are with the selection. If necessary, model the thinking process.

Write the information on your organizer.

You may write words or sentences or draw quick sketches with labels.

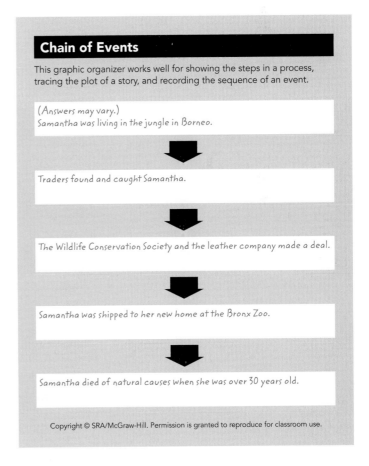

Chain of Events

This graphic organizer works well for showing the steps in a process, tracing the plot of a story, and recording the sequence of an event.

(Answers may vary.)
Samantha was living in the jungle in Borneo.

Traders found and caught Samantha.

The Wildlife Conservation Society and the leather company made a deal.

Samantha was shipped to her new home at the Bronx Zoo.

Samantha died of natural causes when she was over 30 years old.

A Safe Haven

from A Pelican Swallowed My Head and Other Zoo Stories by Edward R. Ricciuti

Deep in the jungles of Borneo, a huge island that lies off the coast of Southeast Asia, a great snake prowls the forest floor. She is a reticulated python, and her ancient ancestors, which looked very much like her, slid through green jungles at the end of the dinosaur age. *Reticulated* is a word that means "having markings like a net," and the skin of a reticulated python is indeed marked with bronzy patches, outlined in black, that resemble netting. This pattern helps the snake blend into the shadows, leaves, and other foliage on the jungle floor, where it lives and hunts.

The python travels slowly forward by flexing two sets of powerful muscles. One set raises scales on her belly, in ripple fashion from head to tail, and as these scales grip the ground another set of muscles pulls the python ahead. She moves silently, except for an occasional rustle of brush or leaves. She is a very large snake, and it is her size that eventually saves her life and leads her to her new home at the Bronx Zoo. There she will be known as Samantha, one of the many animals the zoo has rescued from an uncertain, even deadly, future. And while Samantha may not know it, the zoo has become not only her home, but also her own personal safe haven.

Samantha's Tale

A week or so before, back in the Bornean jungle, Samantha had finally digested her last dinner of a mouse deer, but she was still hungry. A mouse deer stands a foot high at the shoulder and weighs about ten pounds. But this is only a snack for a large python, which sometimes swallows animals, such as wild pigs, weighing in the neighborhood of one hundred pounds, and Samantha needed something more to eat. But Samantha was not the only hunter in the steaming tropical forest. Others, on two legs, were also on the prowl. They were the leather traders, hunting snakes for their skins. The same reticulated pattern that camouflaged Samantha and helped her survive also put her in great danger at the hands of humans. Her glossy skin could be converted into beautiful and expensive boots, belts, handbags, and other leather accessories.

Our story began in Southeast Asia. In what country? Where in Borneo? The main character of the article lived there. Who is the main character? I am going to write that in the first box.

The traders, about a half dozen of them, were fanned out on the forest floor. Experienced jungle hands, they scanned the branches of the smaller trees scattered among the jungle giants. They knew that some snakes, including pythons, often ascend trees in search of prey, but they also surveyed the ground, which was shaded by the green roof of leaves above. When a movement on the forest floor caught the eye of one trader, he turned to look and gasped. The python at his feet was bigger than any snake he had ever seen before.

"There!" he whispered to his companions, but when they saw the python, their eyes widened. Here was a prize, indeed. Moving slowly, they encircled the python, preparing for a rush. Samantha, sensing that something was not right, turned her head from side to side, flicking her tongue out to sense their position, but it was too late. "Pin it down," one yelled. "But watch out for its teeth," hollered another. This was quite a warning—pythons are not venomous, but they have large, curved teeth that can deliver a horrendous bite. The traders took out nooses and snake sticks, designed to pin a snake to the ground, and although Samantha thrashed and hissed, it was no use. She was a captive and her doom was certainly sealed.

It was December 18, 1991, and winter was approaching. The leaves on the oaks, maples, and tulip trees that make the Bronx Zoo a wooded oasis in the city had fallen. A chilly, late autumn wind rattled the branches, and wild ducks splashed down in the zoo's waterfowl ponds. Some were heading south, and for them the ponds were a welcome stopover, while others were zoo ducks that were mingling with the visitors from far away. In the zoo's reptile and amphibians building, which is known as the World of Reptiles, supervisor Bill Holmstrom was looking at a letter. He and the keepers who work under him feed the animals, clean their enclosures, and watch over their general well-being. Bill and his keepers also assist the scientific staff in their efforts to breed reptiles and amphibians in captivity. As Bill began to read the letter he realized it had come from a leather company in Wisconsin. The letter explained that the company's representatives in Borneo had captured a huge python, which was being housed in an abandoned railroad boxcar. They claimed that the python they had captured was immense, and photographs of the snake were enclosed with the letter.

Who found Samantha and what did they do with her? I'll write that in the next box.

Since the early 1900s the Wildlife Conservation Society had had a standing reward that is now $50,000 for anyone who could deliver a live, healthy snake thirty or more feet in length, so the leather company was sure that their python was a candidate for the prize.

What did the people who captured Samantha decide to do with her? How were they going to accomplish that? I'll write that in the next box.

Over the years a handful of people had tried to claim the reward; however, none of their snakes quite measured up. It is very easy to overestimate the length of a large snake, but it is also very difficult to measure one. A snake more than fifteen feet in length is so strong that even a dozen strong men cannot straighten it out without kinks. Its body is continually contracting and squirming, and the more its holders struggle, the harder the snake fights, making the measuring job tougher. So, needless to say, most measurements are at least slightly off the mark. The interesting fact, however, was that the snake described in the letter was a reticulated python, and this was very intriguing to Bill and his boss, John Behler, the curator of the Reptile Department.

The reticulated python is one of the top two candidates for the title of the world's largest snake. The other is the anaconda of South America, and like the python, the anaconda kills its prey by constriction. For centuries there have been reports filtering out of the jungles about reticulated pythons and anacondas that are well over thirty feet long, but none have been fully accepted by scientists. This is not to say that these snakes never exceed thirty feet, as many scientists believe they may. In fact, a python supposedly thirty-two feet long was killed many years ago on the island of Sulawesi, not far from Borneo, and engineers probing the jungles of South America once reported that they had shot an anaconda that was thirty-seven feet long. But regardless of the stories, a live snake more than thirty feet long has never been provided.

John, Bill and other Wildlife Conservation Society staff members discussed the leather company's offer and decided that even if the snake didn't measure up, bringing it to the Bronx Zoo would surely rescue it from an unpleasant end. Reticulated pythons are becoming scarce in the wild, as the killing for their skins has reduced their numbers. They are also dwindling because the forests in which they live are being destroyed, mainly from lumbering and clearing for development.

"Let's give it a try," said John of the company's offer, but it took more than a year to complete the deal with the leather company. Letters and telephone calls went back and forth for months, and then finally arrangements had to be made for transporting the snake in a sound, healthy condition. International agreements require legal documents for shipping wild animals between countries, so lots of paperwork was involved. Even so, the negotiations took longer than usual. There are suspicions that the leather company was stalling in hopes that the python would grow even larger while it lived in the boxcar and they would win the big Bronx Zoo award. But finally, after waiting and waiting, it was a go. John was all set to travel to Borneo to bring the snake back to the safety of the zoo, but then he realized something: It was Ramadan. Ramadan is the ninth month of the Islamic year and is also a holy time of fasting and penance when many routine activities slow to a halt. Since most people of Borneo are Islamic, the python shipment was going to have to wait.

When Ramadan was over, Samantha was ready to be shipped to her new home at the Bronx Zoo, but John Behler would not be the one who would take her there. He was bound for the island of Madagascar, off the southeastern coast of Africa, where he is an expert on the local animal and plant life. A replacement escort for Samantha had to be found. Luckily, the zoo dispatched a reptile importer from Colorado to pick up the python, and Samantha's trip to New York City went without a hitch. Bill Holmstrom and five of his keepers were there to meet her, and so was Dr. William G. Conway, then president of the Wildlife Conservation Society and director of the Bronx Zoo.

Samantha had been shipped in a large burlap sack inside a wooden crate. But along the way the burlap had rotted, and when the crate was opened, Bill and his keepers found themselves looking at one big python, roaming free in the crate. Moving quickly, they placed a tarpaulin over it, one of the keepers grabbed the python behind the head, and everyone else held on to its body. "She was all we could handle," Bill remembers.

What happened to Samantha next? I'll write that in the next box.

Samantha had become accustomed to captivity and to being handled by people, and although she tried to twist and coil her body, she did not put up a difficult struggle. The keepers stretched her out on the floor as best they could, and Bill and Dr. Conway got onto their hands and knees to measure her. No doubt about it, she was a giant—but as they had thought, she was not the prizewinner. The length of the tape, which was actually just a long cord, indicated that she was only slightly more than twenty-one feet. She also weighed only 150 pounds, which is at least fifty pounds less than expected for a snake her length. She seemed in good shape, however, so the keepers weren't worried.

"We were a bit disappointed that she wasn't as long as reported," says Bill, but even so, she was longer than any python known to be in an American zoo. Back at the reptile house an enclosure had been prepared for Samantha that contained strong tree limbs and rocks she could climb, and visitors would be able to view her through thick glass covering the front of the enclosure.

Follow-up

Samantha died of natural causes on November 21, 2002. She was thought to be over 30 years old. At the time of her death, Samantha was over 26 feet long and weighed 275 pounds. She was one of the zoo's most popular attractions with over a million visitors a year.

How did Samantha spend the rest of her life? I'll write that in the next box.

⑤ Assess Understanding

1. Distribute copies of the graphic organizer.

2. Tell the students to listen to the selection again and make notes about the important sequence of events.

3. Reread the selection.

Animals

Goldiefox and the Three Chickens

FICTION

LESSON MAP

1 Getting Started.

2 Read the selection to the group.

3 Present the graphic organizer.

4 Read the selection to the group while working with them to use the graphic organizer.

5 Assess understanding.

MATERIALS

Graphic Organizer #2—Character Qualities: displayed on an overhead; a copy for each student

Related Web sites: http://www.ucalgary.ca/~dkbrown/fft.html
http://www.grimmfairytales.com/en/main

1 Getting Started

BACKGROUND

1. One of the best ways to get hesitant writers started is with "fractured fairy tales" and song parodies. Of course, good parodies require considerable writing talent, but most people can create them well enough to entertain themselves. The Rocky and Bullwinkle fractured fairy tales are classics, and many of them are available on the Internet and at video stores.

VOCABULARY

Present the vocabulary words, using this format:

Irate is an adjective that means **very angry.** What is **irate?** *Irate is an adjective that means very angry.*

Listen. **Goldiefox became irate when he was hungry.** Say that. *Goldiefox became irate when he was hungry.*

convenient *adjective,* handy, nearby. *He hid in a convenient cupboard on the stair landing.*

assume *verb,* take for granted. *Why do you assume it was a man?*

henpeck *verb,* nag, pick on. *"I'll henpeck to within an inch of his life anyone who's in there," scolded Mama Hen.*

2 Read the Selection

1. Explain to the students that this is a parody, a spoof, of a well-known fairy tale, "Goldilocks and the Three Bears." The first reading should be presented with minimal interruption. If a student does ask a question, answer it and continue reading.

2. After presenting the selection, present the graphic organizer.

3 Present the Graphic Organizer

1. Display the graphic organizer, and explain that this kind of organizer can help us describe a character's personality.

2. Explain to the students that they will work through the organizer with you.

4 Use the Graphic Organizer

Reread the selection in sections, and ask questions that will help the students learn about the main character. Suggestions are with the selection. If necessary, model the thinking process.

Write the information on your organizer.

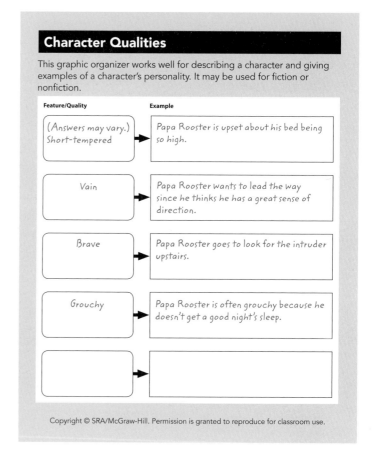

Character Qualities

This graphic organizer works well for describing a character and giving examples of a character's personality. It may be used for fiction or nonfiction.

Feature/Quality	Example
(Answers may vary.) Short-tempered	Papa Rooster is upset about his bed being so high.
Vain	Papa Rooster wants to lead the way since he thinks he has a great sense of direction.
Brave	Papa Rooster goes to look for the intruder upstairs.
Grouchy	Papa Rooster is often grouchy because he doesn't get a good night's sleep.

Goldiefox and the Three Chickens

from Leaping Beauty
by Gregory Maguire

There were once three chickens who lived in a house in the forest.

Papa Rooster was vain and short-tempered. Mama Hen was soothing and patient. Baby Chick was tired of being the littlest one all the time. "Why don't you go to the store?" he used to say to Mama Hen. "Can you buy me a new little brother or sister?"

One morning all three chickens woke up in a bad mood.

Papa Rooster said, "My bed is so high, I almost fell on my beak jumping off the mattress this morning."

Mama Hen said, "Poor thing. My bed is so low, while I was sleeping I rolled right off it and smack into my knitting needles."

Baby Chick said, "You think you have troubles! My bed is too small! I'm bumping into the headboard and the footboard! I need a new one! I know: Why don't we look in a catalog and order a new baby? Then we could give my little baby bed to my new brother or sister."

"I'll think about it, dear," said Mama Hen, which Baby Chick knew full well really meant, *Not very likely in this lifetime, honey chile.*

Mama Hen made some oatmeal and brought it to the table.

"Yikes, it's piping hot!" yelled Papa Rooster.

"So is mine," wailed Baby Chick.

"What a pair of complainers," said Mama Hen. "So blow on it to cool it down already."

"I prefer to save my breath for complaining," said Papa Rooster.

> Here are three of the main characters in the story. Let's choose one of them and list what we find out as we read the story.

Baby Chick blew on his breakfast a little too hard, and then Papa Rooster had something to complain about. He didn't enjoy oatmeal on his coxcomb.

After they had all cleaned up, Mama Hen said, "Why don't we go for a walk in the forest and give the oatmeal a chance to cool down? Ourselves, too."

"I'll lead the way, as I'm the largest and most important," crowed Papa Rooster. "Also I have a wonderful sense of direction."

"I'll follow along behind, as I'm the last, the smallest, worth nothing at all," whimpered Baby Chick. "I wish I had a baby brother or sister chick that I could be bigger than. Let's hunt for one in the ferns."

"I'll go to the park and feed the ducks by myself if you two don't quit your bellyaching," said Mama Hen. And off they went into the woods, single file.

They were gone a long time because Papa Rooster's sense of direction wasn't quite as wonderful as he thought.

Now, who should come slinking through the woods from the other direction but a golden fox. He was beautiful to behold, shiny as the foil around fancy chocolates. But he was miserable, for he had just been fired from his job as a carpenter for a local furniture store. It seemed that a lot of the customers were scared to order rocking chairs for their grannies or cradles for their new babies from a fox who was walking around with a sharp-toothed saw. Besides, he had sharp teeth of his own, which were big and in very good condition. Customers didn't like to come inside the shop.

The out-of-work carpenter—whose name was Goldiefox—was in a bad mood when he came upon the house of the three chickens. He smelled the smell of something delicious. He knocked on the door to ask if he could have a bite, for he was very hungry. When no one answered, he pushed the door open and looked inside. He saw the table with three bowls of oatmeal. "My word!" he said. "A delicious breakfast, and no one here to eat it."

Think of a word to describe [character's name]. Bossy? Silly? Whiney? What did [character's name] do to show us that?

Here's another character to add. In the regular story, "Goldilocks and the Three Bears," which character would this one be?

Goldiefox took a spoonful of oatmeal from the largest bowl. "It is too hot," he said, and moved on to the medium-sized bowl. "It is too cold," he said. The smallest bowl had only a little oatmeal at the bottom, as most of it seemed to have been blown out all over the tablecloth. "This is just right," said Goldiefox, and ate what little there was. But he was still hungry, and he was still cross.

He went into the next room looking for a pie or a sandwich or something. There he saw three chairs. "Perhaps I'll take a rest and wait for the owners of this house to come home," he said to himself. He sat down on the largest chair. It was too hard. By now Goldiefox was thoroughly annoyed, and though he ought to have counted to ten and had a time-out, he lost his temper. He jumped up and down on the large, hard chair, and he broke it.

He then sat in the medium-sized chair. It was too soft. He jumped up and down on it and broke it, too.

There was a small chair. Goldiefox tried to sit in it, but it was too small. Then he tried to jump up and down on it and break it, but it got stuck on his foot. It was a *very* small chair.

"This is not a good day," said Goldiefox to himself. "First I get fired from my job, then I get my foot stuck in a tiny chair. What next?"

Since the family still wasn't showing up, Goldiefox clumped upstairs to try to find a saw with which to remove the small chair from his foot. He found no work tools, but he did see a very high bed.

Since he was tired from all his jumping up and down and breaking furniture, he decided to have a nap. He tried to leap up on the high bed, and he smashed his face on the headboard and broke off a front tooth. We all have days like this sometimes.

Goldiefox became irate. He jumped up and down on the high bed and he broke it.

Next he found a very low bed. It was so low that it was hard to jump up and down and break, so he threw it out the window.

Finally he found an exceedingly small bed. It was clearly too small for a fox to sleep in, but by now he was out of control. Goldiefox tried to jump up and down on it and break it, but the very small bed got stuck on his other foot.

Just at that moment the chicken family came home from their walk.

They were in bad moods. Papa Rooster pretended he hadn't gotten lost. Mama Hen pretended she couldn't hear any whining and walked straight into the kitchen. Baby Chick pretended he belonged to another family and had nine brothers and sisters.

Goldiefox heard them coming. Quite suddenly he found himself ashamed of his bad behavior. He hid in a convenient cupboard on the stair landing.

Papa Rooster looked in his bowl and said, "I'm ready for breakfast, but it looks as if someone has been eating my oatmeal."

Mama Hen came out of the kitchen and looked in her bowl. "Someone has been eating *my* oatmeal," she said.

Baby Chick said, "Someone has been eating my oatmeal, whatever I didn't blow all over the room by mistake! And there's nothing left for me!"

"What kind of loony would break into our house and eat our oatmeal?" said Papa Rooster. "Let us investigate. I'll go first as I'm the strongest and the bravest."

"I'll go last as I'm the weakest and the least important," said Baby Chick, for once glad to be the smallest.

"I'll call the cops," said Mama Hen. "Let the professionals do their jobs."

Papa Rooster strutted into the parlor. "Someone has been sitting in my chair! And he's jumped up and down on it and broken it!"

"Why do you assume it's a he?" said Mama Hen. "Maybe it's a she. I sometimes feel like jumping up and down on things and breaking them. But I choose to control my temper when I feel like that. It's my best quality, patience."

Then she saw her own chair and lost her patience. "Someone's been jumping up and down on my chair, and she's broken it!" she clucked, flabbergasted. "Though, thinking it over some more, it's probably a he."

"Someone's been jumping up and down on *my* chair," screamed Baby Chick, "and I can't even tell if it's *broken* because it isn't even *here* anymore."

"This is serious," said Papa Rooster. "Everybody stay back. I'm going to look upstairs. I have a feeling whoever has done these foul deeds is still here."

"Oooh, I'm scared," said Baby Chick. "This is better than a horror movie."

Papa Rooster climbed the stairs to the bedrooms. Mama Hen and Baby Chick huddled close behind him.

"Somebody has been sleeping in my bed, and he jumped up and down on it and broke it!" cried Papa Rooster. "Not that I care very much. That bed is so high, it makes me dizzy trying to get down in the morning."

"That's why you're always in such a bad mood," clucked Mama Hen. "If you had a better night's sleep, dear, you wouldn't be such a grouch all the time." She then looked for her bed. "My word! Someone's been sleeping on my bed, and it isn't even here!"

"There it is," said Baby Chick, looking out the window. "It's in the garden, squashing the squashes."

"If I catch that vandal, I'll give him a piece of my mind!" squawked Mama Hen. "Clearly he doesn't have any of his own."

What more have we learned about the character? How did he/she act after discovering that someone had broken into the house? What are some examples?

"Why do you assume it's a he?" asked Papa Rooster, but Mama Hen was giving him such a look that he didn't wait for an answer.

"Someone's been jumping up and down on *my* bed, and it's probably broken or thrown out the window, but I can't even *find* it!" cried Baby Chick.

"We have problems with our furniture," said Papa Rooster.

"Do you think it could be ghosts?" said Mama Hen.

"What if it's hiding in the convenient cupboard on the stair landing?" screeched Baby Chick.

His parents looked at him.

"Well, that's where *I* hide when *I* do something wrong," he said.

The three chickens approached the door to the convenient cupboard on the stair landing. "Stand back," said Papa Rooster. "I'll fling the door open with a bold and decisive gesture."

"I'll henpeck to within an inch of his life anyone who's in there," scolded Mama Hen.

"Maybe it's a new baby brother or sister for *me*!" cried Baby Chick.

"Son, we have to have a little chat," said Papa Rooster. "However convenient a cupboard is, it's not where new baby brothers and sisters come from." He flung open the door.

Goldiefox, who had been trembling in terror at the sound of the furious chickens, stumbled out onto the landing. He tried to run away, but with a tiny bed on one foot and a tiny chair on the other, he merely tumbled to the bottom of the stairs.

In an instant the three chickens had launched themselves through the air and tackled him. Papa Rooster sat on his head. Mama Hen sat on his tail. Baby Chick ran round in the front and looked him in the eye.

"I can smell oatmeal on his breath!" he shouted. "This is our villain!"

"How dare you jump up and down on our furniture and break it!" cried Papa Rooster. "Would you like me to jump up and down on your head and break *that*?"

"How dare you throw my bed out the window!" cried Mama Hen. "Would you like me to throw you out the window?"

"How dare you eat my oatmeal, after I had blown on it to cool it down!" cried Baby Chick. "Would you like me to blow on you to cool *you* down?" Without waiting for an answer, he made good on his threat.

"Please," said Goldiefox, "please. Dear chickens of the woods. I have been a bad fox. I have done everything wrong. I am out of work, I am hungry, and I have miniature furniture stuck to my feet. Furthermore I have broken a tooth as well as most of your furniture. This is not one of my good days. Do not jump up and down on me. Do not throw me out the window. And stop blowing in my face; it's very annoying."

Baby Chick stopped.

"I will tell you something," said Goldiefox. "If you let me live with you, I will build you all new furniture. The chairs will not be too hard or too soft or too little. The bed will not be too high or too low or too little. Perhaps I can set up shop in the backyard and make furniture there, away from the prying eyes of animals too frightened to buy furniture from me. You can sell it in your front room."

"Well, perhaps," said Papa Rooster. "I wouldn't be in such a bad mood if I could get a better night's sleep."

"If you got a better night's sleep, we'd *all* get a better night's sleep," said Mama Hen. "I think it's a great idea. Perhaps I'll make up batches of oatmeal and we can have an oatmeal restaurant, too. For all the customers who come to buy furniture."

What more have we learned about [character's name]? How did he/she act after capturing the fox? What are some examples?

"But where will you sleep?" asked Baby Chick.

"I can sleep in the convenient cupboard on the stair landing," said Goldiefox.

And that's just what they did. They opened a new store in the woods, called The Three Chickens Furniture Store and Oatmeal Restaurant. Every once in a while the oatmeal was too hot to eat, so the chickens went for a walk in the woods. But they left Goldiefox behind to guard their house. With his broken front tooth, he was quite a scary-looking animal. So they never had trouble with hungry, destructive trespassers again.

Baby Chick never *did* get a baby brother or sister. But at the end of the day, when the carpenter tools were all stored away, Goldiefox would wash his face of sawdust and play with Baby Chick.

They especially enjoyed jumping on the furniture, now that it was strong enough to stand up to such punishment.

5 Assess Understanding

1. Distribute copies of the graphic organizer.

2. Tell the students to listen to the selection again and make notes about one character in the story.

3. Reread the selection.

Baseball

Casey at the Bat

FICTION

LESSON MAP

1 Getting Started.

2 Read the selection to the group.

3 Present the graphic organizer.

4 Read the selection to the group while working with them to use the graphic organizer.

5 Assess understanding.

MATERIALS

- Graphic Organizer #1—Story Elements: displayed on an overhead; a copy for each student

- Related Web sites: http://www.baseball-almanac.com/poetry/po_case.shtml
http://www.baseballhalloffame.org/

1 Getting Started

BACKGROUND

1. Ernest Thayer was a Harvard philosophy graduate and classmate of William Randolph Hearst's. When Hearst acquired the *San Francisco Examiner,* he hired Thayer to write a humorous column. Thayer wrote under the pen name "Phin." In 1888, he wrote the narrative poem "Casey at the Bat," and it was published in the *Examiner* on June 3, 1888. The poem became famous when De Wolf Hopper, a popular comedian, began performing it in his shows. A recording of Hopper's reading is on the Baseball Almanac Web site.

2. There are several versions of the poem, with minor word variations. It is believed that this version is the original published version.

VOCABULARY

Present the vocabulary words, using this format:

Melancholy is an adjective that means **sadness, unhappiness.** What is **melancholy?** *Melancholy is a noun that means sadness, unhappiness.*

Listen. **The team was losing, and an air of melancholy settled over the ball park.** Say that. *The team was losing, and an air of melancholy settled over the ball park.*

haughty *adjective,* stuck-up, self-important. *His haughty attitude surrounded him as he walked down the hall.*

visage *noun,* features, face. *His visage revealed his pride.*

2 Read the Selection

1. Explain to the students that this is a narrative poem—it tells a story. The first reading should be presented with minimal interruption. If a student does ask a question, answer it and continue reading.

2. After reading the selection, ask the students, What lesson do you think mighty Casey learned that day?

3 Present the Graphic Organizer

1. Display the graphic organizer, and explain that this kind of organizer can help us figure out and remember the story elements of a narrative poem.

2. Explain to the students that they will work through the organizer with you.

4 Use the Graphic Organizer

Read the selection in sections, and ask questions that will help the students identify the story elements. Suggestions are with the selection. If necessary, model the thinking process.

Write the information on your organizer.

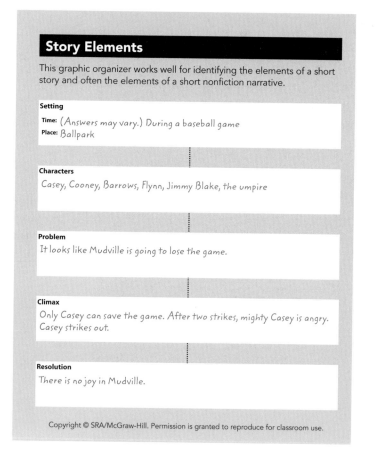

Story Elements

This graphic organizer works well for identifying the elements of a short story and often the elements of a short nonfiction narrative.

Setting
Time: *(Answers may vary.) During a baseball game*
Place: *Ballpark*

Characters
Casey, Cooney, Barrows, Flynn, Jimmy Blake, the umpire

Problem
It looks like Mudville is going to lose the game.

Climax
Only Casey can save the game. After two strikes, mighty Casey is angry. Casey strikes out.

Resolution
There is no joy in Mudville.

Casey at the Bat

By Ernest Lawrence Thayer
Taken From the San Francisco Examiner—June 3, 1888

The story takes place in a ballpark. If you know sports, you can figure that out easily. If you don't, you might not figure it out. What are the clues to the setting?

The problem? It looks like Mudville is going to lose the game. The fans seem to think only one person can save the game. Several characters have been mentioned, but Casey is the star, the most important character. Listen to two verses again for clues. Then listen to the rest of the poem to find out what kind of person Casey is.

Here comes the hero—mighty Casey. At this point, the story starts building to the climax. This is the most exciting part of the situation.

The outlook wasn't brilliant for the Mudville nine that day;
The score stood four to two, with but one inning more to play.
And then when Cooney died at first, and Barrows did the same,
A pall-like silence fell upon the patrons of the game.

A straggling few got up to go in deep despair. The rest
Clung to that hope which springs eternal in the human breast;
They thought, "If only Casey could but get a whack at that—
We'd put up even money now, with Casey at the bat."

But Flynn preceded Casey, as did also Jimmy Blake,
And the former was a lulu, while the latter was a cake;
So upon that stricken multitude grim melancholy sat;
For there seemed but little chance of Casey's getting to the bat.

But Flynn let drive a single, to the wonderment of all,
And Blake, the much despised, tore the cover off the ball;
And when the dust had lifted, and men saw what had occurred,
There was Jimmy safe at second and Flynn a-hugging third.

Then from five thousand throats and more there rose a lusty yell;
It rumbled through the valley, it rattled in the dell;
It knocked upon the mountain and recoiled upon the flat,
For Casey, mighty Casey, was advancing to the bat.

There was ease in Casey's manner as he stepped into his place;
There was pride in Casey's bearing and a smile on Casey's face.
And when, responding to the cheers, he lightly doffed his hat,
No stranger in the crowd could doubt 'twas Casey at the bat.

Ten thousand eyes were on him as he rubbed his hands with dirt;
Five thousand tongues applauded when he wiped them on his shirt.
Then while the writhing pitcher ground the ball into his hip,
Defiance flashed in Casey's eye, a sneer curled Casey's lip.

And now the leather-covered sphere came hurtling through the air,
And Casey stood a-watching it in haughty grandeur there.
Close by the sturdy batsman the ball unheeded sped—
"That ain't my style," said Casey. "Strike one!" the umpire said.

From the benches, black with people, there went up a muffled roar,
Like the beating of the storm-waves on a stern and distant shore.
"Kill him! Kill the umpire!" shouted someone on the stand;
And it's likely they'd have killed him had not Casey raised his hand.

With a smile of Christian charity great Casey's visage shone;
He stilled the rising tumult; he bade the game go on;
He signaled to the pitcher, and once more the dun sphere flew;
But Casey still ignored it, and the umpire said "Strike two!"

"Fraud!" cried the maddened thousands, and echo answered "Fraud!"
But one scornful look from Casey and the audience was awed.
They saw his face grow stern and cold, they saw his muscles strain,
And they knew that Casey wouldn't let that ball go by again.

The sneer has fled from Casey's lip, the teeth are clenched in hate;
He pounds with cruel violence his bat upon the plate.
And now the pitcher holds the ball, and now he lets it go,
And now the air is shattered by the force of Casey's blow.

Oh, somewhere in this favored land the sun is shining bright,
The band is playing somewhere, and somewhere hearts are light,
And somewhere men are laughing, and somewhere children shout;
But there is no joy in Mudville—mighty Casey has struck out.

> This is the moment. The problem is solved. What happened? What do you think happened after Casey struck out? Why do you think that?

5 Assess Understanding

1. Distribute copies of the graphic organizer.

2. Tell the students to listen to the selection again and make notes about the story elements in the poem.

3. Reread the selection.

Baseball

Clemente Tells the Story of a True Baseball Hero

NON FICTION

LESSON MAP

1 Getting Started.

2 Read the selection to the group.

3 Present the graphic organizer.

4 Read the selection to the group while working with them to use the graphic organizer.

5 Assess understanding.

MATERIALS

- Graphic Organizer #2—Character Qualities: displayed on an overhead; a copy for each student

- Related Web sites: http://www. baseballhalloffame.org/hofers_and_ honorees/hofer_bios/Clemente_Roberto. htm
  http://www.npr.org/templates/story/story. php?storyId=5369849

1 Getting Started

BACKGROUND

1. At the National Public Radio Web site, listed in the box, you can hear this interview, see photos, and read an excerpt of the book *Clemente* by David Maraniss. Because Roberto Clemente is a true baseball hero and a hero to the Latin community, there are many books of all reading levels available.

VOCABULARY

Present the vocabulary words, using this format:

Graceful is an adjective that means **elegant, attractive, showing beauty of movement.** What is **graceful?** *Graceful is an adjective that means elegant, attractive, showing beauty of movement.*

Listen. **Clemente was a graceful man on and off the field.** Say that. *Clemente was a graceful man on and off the field.*

ritual *noun,* tradition, ceremony. *He followed the same ritual each time he was at bat.*

humanitarian *adjective,* kind, caring. *Roberto Clemente died while on a humanitarian mission.*

② Read the Selection

1. Explain to the students that this is a radio interview. The announcer Don Gonyea is interviewing David Maraniss, who has just written a biography of Roberto Clemente.

2. After reading the selection, ask the students, What would you tell others about Roberto Clemente?

③ Present the Graphic Organizer

1. Display the graphic organizer, and explain that this kind of organizer can help us identify and record information about a person's personality and accomplishments.

2. Explain to the students that they will work through the organizer with you.

④ Use the Graphic Organizer

Reread the selection in sections, and ask questions that will help the students learn about Roberto Clemente. Suggestions are with the selection. If necessary, model the thinking process.

Write the information on your organizer.

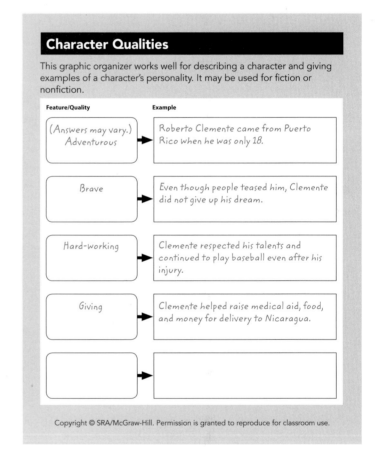

Character Qualities

This graphic organizer works well for describing a character and giving examples of a character's personality. It may be used for fiction or nonfiction.

Feature/Quality	Example
(Answers may vary.) Adventurous	Roberto Clemente came from Puerto Rico when he was only 18.
Brave	Even though people teased him, Clemente did not give up his dream.
Hard-working	Clemente respected his talents and continued to play baseball even after his injury.
Giving	Clemente helped raise medical aid, food, and money for delivery to Nicaragua.

Clemente Tells the Story of a True Baseball Hero
from April 30, 2006 Interview on National Public Radio

DON GONYEA, host: Look down the lineup of any Major League Baseball team, and you'll find a roster full of names like Rodriguez and Rivera and Pujols and Ortiz. Each owes a debt to baseball's very first Latin American superstar, Roberto Clemente, who played 18 seasons for the Pittsburgh Pirates, his entire career. Clemente was a graceful presence on the diamond, making near-impossible plays in the outfield and winning four National League batting titles.

(Soundbite of baseball game)
GONYEA: That hit, number 3,000, was Clemente's last. He died three months later in a plane crash carrying relief supplies he had collected for victims of a deadly earthquake in Nicaragua on New Year's Eve in 1972. David Maraniss is a Pulitzer Prize-winning journalist who's written books about former President Bill Clinton and Green Bay Packers coach Vince Lombardi. His latest work is *Clemente: The Passion and Grace of Baseball's Last Hero.*

David Maraniss joins us from our studios in New York. Welcome.

Mr. DAVID MARANISS (Author, *Clemente*): Thank you, Don. Great to be with you.

GONYEA: Well, let's go back to the beginning. What was it like for a young ball player like Clemente, 18 years old or so, coming to the US to play baseball in the mid-1950s? Jackie Robinson had already broken the color barrier, but were there other barriers he encountered?

Mr. MARANISS: Absolutely. Remember, he came from Puerto Rico, which I think all societies have certain racism, but there was no segregation in Puerto Rico. The great Negro League players from the US would go down to the Puerto Rico to play before they could play in the United States. So Clemente came from a place where being a black Latino was not a bar to anything.

The first thing we discover about Roberto is that he came from Puerto Rico when he was 18 years old. He was a black Latino. What do those facts tell us about the kind of person he was? He was brave. He was adventurous. He must have been a good ballplayer.

He came to Pittsburgh, had no Latin community whatsoever. For many, many years the sportswriters would quote him in broken English. You know, there was a big headline that said, I get heet, when he got the winning hit in an All Star game instead of hit, H-E-E-T. It infuriated Clemente.

Here are a few more things that tell us he was brave and determined. Some people made fun of his English, and it made him angry, but he didn't give up his dream.

And so the adjustment took a long time for Clemente, but he did it. And one of the great testaments is that Pittsburgh, sort of the quintessential blue-collar steel town, you know, white ethnic dominant, came to love Roberto Clemente.

GONYEA: I'd like to ask you to read a passage from the book, page 187, about how seriously Clemente took every single aspect of the game, including every single at bat.

Mr. MARANISS (Reading): Clemente would never smile preparing for a plate appearance. When he approached the rack inside the dugout, his attitude was that of a surgeon toward his instruments, or a toreador toward his swords. He knew these bats, these (unintelligible) models. He had studied them from the moment a new shipment came in during spring training. He was as tuned to them as he was to his body.

And his choice might depend on his mood or the fitness of his lower back or the pitcher on the mound, or something he saw in the grain of wood. Not ready yet to decide, he would haul two or three bats out to the on-deck circle, carrying them all in one hand, then he would kneel, left knee bent at 90 degrees, right knee touching the ground, posture erect, the bats draped elegantly against his thigh.

One by one he would pick them up, heft them, as he stared at the pitcher and wiped them with his rag. Here was the serenity of Clemente before the storm.

GONYEA: You're describing a ritual and the ritual continued with the walk to the plate, right? As he kind of stretched and worked the kinks out?

GONYEA: He was already a national hero in Puerto Rico prior to this, but his death on a humanitarian mission really took it to another level, didn't it?

Mr. MARANISS: One of the great writers in Puerto Rico said that on the night of his death, his immortality began. The next morning thousands of people lined the beach near where the plane went down thinking that Clemente might walk out of the sea.

GONYEA: David Maraniss is the author of *Clemente: The Passion and Grace of Baseball's Last Hero*. Thanks so much for joining us.

Mr. MARANISS: Thank you, Don.

GONYEA: There's a photographic timeline of Roberto Clemente's career at our Web site, NPR.org.
(Soundbite of music)

5 Assess Understanding

1. Distribute copies of the graphic organizer.
2. Tell the students to listen to the selection again and make notes about Roberto Clemente.
3. Reread the selection.

Baseball

Lesson 9
Women's Baseball

NON FICTION

LESSON MAP

1. Getting Started.
2. Read the selection to the group.
3. Present the graphic organizer.
4. Read the selection to the group while working with them to use the graphic organizer.
5. Assess understanding.

MATERIALS

- Graphic Organizer #3—Chain of Events: displayed on an overhead; a copy for each student
- Related Web sites: http://www.baseballhalloffame.org/education/primary_sources/women/index.htm
  http://www.awbf.org

1 Getting Started

BACKGROUND

1. Women's baseball has a history of its own. This selection takes readers from women's first baseball games to the creation of the modern American Women's Baseball Federation.

VOCABULARY

Present the vocabulary words, using this format:

Surreptitiously is an adverb that means **secretly.** What is **surreptitiously?** *Surreptitiously is an adverb that means secretly.*

Listen. **He surreptitiously lifted the corner of the display cabinet.** Say that. *He surreptitiously lifted the corner of the display cabinet.*

barnstorm *verb,* to travel from place to place, usually in rural areas. *Because he was running for president, the candidate barnstormed through the Midwest.*

dwindling *adjective,* gradually becoming smaller or less. *There was a dwindling crowd after the festivities.*

garner *verb,* to earn, collect. *The ice-cream parlor garnered high profits, despite the cold weather.*

② Read the Selection

1. The first reading should be presented with minimal interruption. If a student does ask a question, answer it and continue reading.

2. After presenting the selection, present the graphic organizer.

③ Present the Graphic Organizer

1. Display the graphic organizer, and explain that this kind of organizer can help us record a chain of events.

2. Explain to the students that they will work through the organizer with you.

④ Use the Graphic Organizer

Reread the selection in sections, and ask questions that will help the students track the chain of events in the article. Suggestions are with the selection. If necessary, model the thinking process.

Write the information on your organizer.

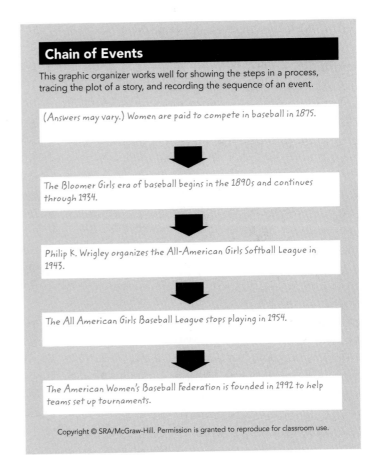

Chain of Events

This graphic organizer works well for showing the steps in a process, tracing the plot of a story, and recording the sequence of an event.

(Answers may vary.) Women are paid to compete in baseball in 1875.

The Bloomer Girls era of baseball begins in the 1890s and continues through 1934.

Philip K. Wrigley organizes the All-American Girls Softball League in 1943.

The All American Girls Baseball League stops playing in 1954.

The American Women's Baseball Federation is founded in 1992 to help teams set up tournaments.

Women's Baseball
by Elise Luxembourg

When you think of baseball, what comes to mind? You might think of a game you played in or went to. Perhaps you know something about the history of baseball and the first professional baseball team, the Cincinnati Red Stockings. But did you know that women's baseball has a history of its own?

Although the first women's baseball team was organized earlier at Vassar College, women were not actually paid to compete until 1875. At that time, three men organized a baseball club for women and charged admission for people to see the Blondes play the Brunettes. These first games were not very serious—they were probably more of an attempt to garner new interest in the sport—but women caught on and liked the game.

In the early stages of women's baseball, women wore up to thirty pounds of clothing! Their first outfits included floor-length skirts, high-buttoned shoes, and long-sleeved blouses. Amelia Bloomer, a women's rights activist, created loose-fitting pants based on Turkish design, and these "bloomers" made it easier for women to move freely, especially in baseball. Suddenly, Bloomer Girls baseball teams started organizing across the United States.

The period from the 1890s through 1934 is known as the Bloomer Girls era of baseball. The Bloomer Girls teams barnstormed across the country, challenging local and even minor league men's teams. Each Bloomer Girls team usually had at least one male member, and the Bloomer Girls teams won many of the competitive games they played. For a short period, there were hundreds of these teams, and women had the opportunity to travel and work simultaneously. However, the last team stopped playing in 1934 because public opinion considered women's athletic abilities inferior to those of men.

What major event happened in 1875 in women's baseball? That's the first step in the chain of events.

A new era developed in baseball that was named after a type of women's pants. What was this era called? That's the second step in the chain of events . . .

The onset of World War II encouraged the development of a new women's league. What was this league called? That's the third step in the chain.

In 1943, Philip K. Wrigley organized the All-American Girls Softball League. At the time, many major league baseball players were out of the country, taking part in World War II. This new women's league was a way for the country to still enjoy its pastime. There were many differences, however, between previous baseball and this new league—for example, the diamond and ball used were different sizes, and women were required to wear skirts during the games. Women were expected to act proper at all times.

The fourth step in the chain explains what eventually happened to the All-American Girls Baseball League.

Although the team started as a softball league, it evolved into fast-pitched softball and then baseball over its first decade. Eventually, the league became the All-American Girls Baseball League. They stopped playing in 1954 due to men returning home after the war, available to play baseball again. The audience was also dwindling due to other forms of entertainment (television, for example) being more readily available to the public.

After the All-American Girls Baseball League disbanded, there was little opportunity for women to play professional baseball. In 1952, twenty-four-year-old Eleanor Engels was signed by a minor league team, the Harrisburg Senators. However, she never had the chance to play her first game, as her contract was canceled shortly thereafter. Ever since then, women who want to play professionally have resorted to playing softball.

What women's federation provides women the opportunity to play baseball today? That's the fifth step.

Today, several women's baseball associations are developing to help women play baseball. For example, the American Women's Baseball Federation was founded to help organize women's baseball teams in the United States, and this federation has helped teams network and set up tournaments since 1992. It has organized seventeen regional and national tournaments, and they have even established Women's World Series events with international partners.

5 Assess Understanding

1. Distribute copies of the graphic organizer.

2. Tell the students to listen to the selection again and make notes about the chain of events.

3. Reread the selection.

Baseball
A Tale of Two City Kids

NON FICTION

LESSON MAP

1 Getting Started.

2 Read the selection to the group.

3 Present the graphic organizer.

4 Read the selection to the group while working with them to use the graphic organizer.

5 Assess understanding.

MATERIALS

- Graphic Organizer #4—Facts and Feelings/Opinions: displayed on an overhead; a copy for each student

- Related Web sites: http://www.baseballhalloffame.org/
http://www.mannyramirez.com/home.htm
http://boston.redsox.mlb.com

1 Getting Started

BACKGROUND

1. More than anything, Steve Mandl wanted to play professional baseball. It wasn't to be, but he might be the best high school baseball coach in the country. His overall record as of 2006 was 696–92 (.883). And he's coached some of the best; among them are Manny Ramirez, Alex Arias, Jose Antigua, and Manuel Olivera.

VOCABULARY

Present the vocabulary words, using this format:

Ovation is a noun that means **applause.** What is **ovation?** *Ovation is a noun that means applause.*

Listen. **He dreamed of being greeted with a thunderous ovation.** Say that. *He dreamed of being greeted with a thunderous ovation.*

frantically adverb, hysterically, madly. *He was running around frantically looking for a baseball coach.*

2 Read the Selection

1. Before reading the selection, ask students how they prove that something is true. Remind them that we can research in books, on the Internet, talk to experts, and even get information from people with experience. The first reading should be presented with minimal interruption. If a student does ask a question, answer it and continue reading.

2. After reading the selection, present the graphic organizer.

3 Present the Graphic Organizer

1. Display the graphic organizer, and explain that this kind of organizer can help us distinguish facts from feelings and opinions.

2. Explain to the students that they will work through the organizer with you.

4 Use the Graphic Organizer

Reread the selection in sections, and ask questions that will help the students distinguish facts from feelings and opinions. Suggestions are with the selection. If necessary, model the thinking process.

Write the information on your organizer.

Facts and Feelings/Opinions

This graphic organizer works well for distinguishing between facts and opinions.

Facts:
1. (Answers may vary.) Steve Mandel injured his knee.
2. Manny Ramirez came to N.Y. from the Dominican Republic.
3. Ramirez played baseball in the streets with a broomstick.
4. In 8th grade, Ramirez played on the high school team.
5. Ramirez played his first major-league game at Yankee Stadium.

Feelings/Opinions:
1. Life without baseball was life without hope.
2. His new life in America was scary.
3. My friend is really good at baseball.
4. School was hard.
5.

Copyright © SRA/McGraw-Hill. Permission is granted to reproduce for classroom use.

A Tale of Two City Kids

from The Good Guys of Baseball
by Terry Egan, Stan Friedmann, and Mike Levine

Pop. Pop. Smoke and pop.

The kid threw bullets and he knew it. He blew away the toughest hitters on the block. Even gruff, gray-haired Brooklyn men who had seen 'em all knew that this fireballing Bensonhurst boy was the real deal.

"The paper says the kid's got a tryout with the Mets," said one of the old-timers.

Steve Mandl would hear the talking and picture himself a big-league star. He always dreamed of pitching for the Los Angeles Dodgers, palm trees swaying in the distance. A sold-out stadium would be cheering his every strikeout, his friends and family yelling the loudest. Swing and miss, strike three, a no-hitter . . . and Steve Mandl would tip his cap to the thunderous hometown ovation.

Steve was proud he was a good ballplayer. As an outsider in a tough neighborhood, it earned him respect. He was an all-star at basketball, too.

One day he was soaring for a rebound and on his way down he heard an awful sound.

Crack.

The kid had hurt himself and he knew it. His knee was smashed to pieces. He knew he couldn't play baseball anymore. At seventeen, Steve Mandl felt like he'd lost his best friend. He bounced around from job to job. He didn't make much money, the work was boring, and his glory days were gone. Life without baseball was life without hope. In time, he went back to school and became a substitute gym teacher at George Washington High School in New York City. He hated it. He didn't know the kids and they didn't know him. He was about to give it up.

Listen to a statement again: His knee was smashed to pieces. Is that a fact or an opinion? (How could you prove it?) Here's another statement: "Life without baseball was life without hope." Is that a fact or an opinion? (How could you prove it?)

Then, one morning, the principal was running around the halls frantically. The school's baseball coach had suddenly quit.

"Do any teachers here know anything about baseball?"

"I do," said Steve Mandl.

"Who are you?" asked the principal.

~~~~~~~~~~~~~~~~~~~~~~~~~~~~~~~~~~

Pop. Pop. Smoke and pop. Twelve-year-old Manny Ramirez heard the gunshots ring out down his block. His new life in America was scary.

Every day the bullets whizzed by. Every night, the drug dealers took over the streets and peddled their poisons. Manny would fall asleep to the screaming lullaby of police sirens and ambulance wails in his Washington Heights neighborhood.

He had come to New York City from the Dominican Republic. And like so many others from his country, Manny dreamed of becoming a big-time ballplayer. The only problem was Manny didn't have a glove, a bat, or a hardball. His parents didn't have the time or the money. He was on his own.

Manny loved baseball and had to find a game any way he could. He played in the crowded streets with a broomstick and a sponge ball. He hit the ball twice as far as the other kids.

He was strong as an ox and he needed to play with the big guys. That meant trouble, because in this neighborhood, some of the big guys were the most feared drug dealers in New York.

When these players took the field, they played each other for big bucks. It was dirty money, earned from selling crack and heroin to young neighborhood kids. Manny stayed away from drugs but he couldn't stay away from baseball. Word got around that the big kid could hit the ball a mile. The drug dealers stuck him into the lineup.

The kid was matched against grown men. When he hit, the gangsters loved him. But once, when Manny struck out with the bases loaded in the bottom of the ninth, he had to run for his life. He was rescued by the neighborhood of baseball. He found out about a youth league in Brooklyn and traveled an hour each way on the rickety subway just to have a chance to play. Back in his own neighborhood, under dim lights, he played long into the night. Maybe Manny Ramirez didn't have a nickel to his name. So maybe he had to live on the meanest of streets. Maybe he couldn't speak the language of his new homeland.

But he understood baseball. And when he dug into the batter's box of a city park, he planted his roots in America.

~~~~~~~~~~~~~~~~~~~~~~~~

Meanwhile, Manny's friend, a kid named Roberto, a pitcher for the George Washington High School team, was pleading with his coach.

"You gotta check out my friend, Manny. He's only fourteen, but he's really good."

"Forget it," the coach said. "Bring him around next year when he gets to high school."

"No, please," Roberto said. "Check him out now."

When Steve Mandl, baseball coach of George Washington High School, saw a big kid walking across the field, he figured, "This has to be Ramirez."

"Hey, why not give the kid a shot?" thought Mandl. "Looks like he could use a break." Since becoming a coach, Mandl felt at home with his life again. "It used to be all about me," he'd say. "Now it's all about the kids."

"Hey, pal," Mandl said to the shy kid. "I hear you can play ball."

Mandl told Ramirez that he was too young to play on the high school team, but he'd try him out in a few practice games. He worried that young Manny would be overmatched.

Listen again and tell us which things can be proved and how we might prove them. (Reread the paragraph. If necessary, remind students that they can ask Manny.)

Listen carefully for statements that tell about feelings and opinions. I will stop after each sentence. When I read an opinion or feeling, hold up your hand. (Reread the next two paragraphs.)

First time up for Ramirez, crack, base hit. Next time up, double. Boom. Triple. Single. Home run. Double again. Over four games, Ramirez went nine for nine.

"Guess you can play some," Mandl said, smiling.

The next year Ramirez was the star of the team. He belted round-trippers over the fence, but he wasn't home free. The streets wouldn't let go of Manny Ramirez. The drug dealers beheld this big strapping kid and they thought he'd make a good bodyguard.

"Yo, kid," they said. "You want to make some easy money?"

"No," said Ramirez, who didn't have a penny in his pocket.

He was a ballplayer. Every morning Ramirez would get up, strap a spare tire to his back, and run twenty blocks to school to build up his muscles. Coach Mandl would smash ground balls to him until the sun went down. Then he'd buy dinner for the hungry third baseman.

Ramirez still couldn't speak English very well. School was hard and he skipped classes. Mandl heard about it and made sure he showed up.

The next couple of years, Ramirez and Mandl were part of a great New York City story. Together, a bunch of poor kids from mean streets and a broken-down ex-prospect who once soured on life created the sweetest of baseball dreams.

And when George Washington won the city championship, Steve Mandl and Manny Ramirez gave each other a bear hug.

Ramirez was the first-round draft choice of the Cleveland Indians, then baseball's sorriest team over the past fifty years. Within a season, Ramirez made it to the big leagues. His first major-league game was at Yankee Stadium, just across the river from Ramirez's old neighborhood. Just about the whole neighborhood was there to see him. Except for his friend, Roberto, the pitcher who had begged Steve Mandl to give Ramirez a shot. The streets had killed Roberto. Years of living on the edge had taken their toll.

Listen for statements that are facts. I will stop after each sentence. If I read a fact, hold up your hand. (Reread the next two paragraphs.)

When Ramirez took his turn at bat, a roar of desperate hope rang out from his cheering section in the upper deck.

"Manny, Manny, Manny!" they shouted, begging him not to fail.

Crack. The ball rocketed deep into the New York City night. The Yankee outfielders raced back and then just watched, along with the world, as the ball sailed over the big black wall. Home run.

Some say you can still hear the cheers in Washington Heights. You can hear them every time a poor kid swinging a broomstick pretends he's All-Star Manny Ramirez. And you can hear them at George Washington High School, every time Coach Steve Mandl opens another box of baseball cleats donated by Manny Ramirez. These cleats will be running the bases in search of another American dream.

5 Assess Understanding

1. Distribute copies of the graphic organizer.

2. Tell the students to listen to the selection again and make notes to help them remember some of the facts and the opinions.

3. Reread the selection.

Baseball

The North and the Southpaw

FICTION

LESSON MAP

1 Getting Started.

2 Read the selection to the group.

3 Present the graphic organizer.

4 Read the selection to the group while working with them to use the graphic organizer.

5 Assess understanding.

MATERIALS

- Graphic Organizer #5—Cause and Effect: displayed on an overhead; a copy for each student

- Related Web sites: http://oha.ci.alexandria. va.us/fortward/special-sections/baseball/ http://www.rpi.edu/~fiscap/history_files/ history1.htm

1 Getting Started

BACKGROUND

1. Explain to the students that this is a fictional story about a young private in the Union Army during the Civil War, and how he introduced the men in his unit to the game of baseball.

VOCABULARY

Present the vocabulary words, using this format:

Comrade is a noun that means **a friend or companion, a person who shares one's interests.** What is **comrade?** *Comrade is a noun that means a friend or companion, a person who shares one's interests.*

Listen. **Andrew wanted to introduce his comrades to the game of baseball.** Say that. *Andrew wanted to introduce his comrades to the game of baseball.*

2 Read the Selection

1. The first reading should be presented with minimal interruption. If a student does ask a question, answer it and continue reading.

2. After reading the selection, ask the students, What was the problem the men faced in this story? How did Andrew help come up with a solution to the problem?

3 Present the Graphic Organizer

1. Display the graphic organizer, and explain that this kind of organizer can help sort out causes and effects.

2. Explain to the students that they will work through the organizer with you.

4 Use the Graphic Organizer

Reread the selection in sections, and ask questions that will help the students identify cause and effect. Suggestions are with the selection. If necessary, model the thinking process.

Write the information on your organizer.

Cause and Effect

This graphic organizer works well for showing simple cause and effect. By adding relationship arrows, you can also use it to show a chain of cause and effect, multiple effects from a single cause, or multiple causes with a single effect.

Cause (Why)

(Answers may vary.)
1. It was too hot to sleep.
2. The men had many long hours to fill.
3. There was little to do.
4. The camp offered no luxuries.

Effect (What)

1. Andrew shared the game of baseball with his men.
2. The men formed teams and set up a baseball diamond.
3. Baseball became so popular that the men organized games with other units.
4. Andrew earned the nickname "The Southpaw."
5. Baseball grew in popularity among units fighting for the North and the South.

The North and the Southpaw
by Marie Mackey

Andrew Carver awoke early in his tent. It was too hot and sticky to sleep. There was no wind and the sun had already risen in the east, sending hot rays down on the Union Army camp in Nashville, Tennessee. It was 1862 and the Union Army of the North was battling the Confederate Army of the South in the U.S. Civil War.

Andrew stretched and wiped the sweat from his forehead with his shirtsleeve. Slowly, he made his way to the center of camp, where he could smell the New England corn cakes that were being prepared for breakfast. Although it was only 6:00 AM, Andrew found that most of the camp was already awake. He guessed it was too hot for anyone to sleep.

Andrew's unit was waiting for orders from General Grant. Since there were no telephones or radios, it could take a long time to get messages from one camp to another. The men had many long hours to fill.

There was little to do, and the camp offered no luxuries. Some men had a favorite book with them, that they read over and over again. Others passed the time writing letters home. Although they did not know it at the time, these men would soon come to enjoy the excitement of a game called baseball.

As he ate his corn cakes, Andrew noticed a few of his fellow soldiers tossing a rawhide ball across a nearby field. This made him think about his boyhood friend, John Frederickson. John's family had moved to Andrew's hometown of Alliance, Ohio from New York City. In New York, John had been involved in local baseball clubs and had developed a love of the game. Upon moving to Ohio, he taught his new friends, one of whom was Andrew Carver, to play.

Andrew decided he would share the game of baseball with the men in his unit. Finishing his breakfast and brushing the corn cake crumbs from his hands, he began looking for a branch of just the right thickness and weight. After examining several, Andrew found one that satisfied him.

As he sat in the soft grass beneath a large, old shade tree, he began to whittle. Working the fresh, green wood in his hands, Andrew carved out one large, rounded end and one narrow end.

The men in this Civil War army camp have a problem. Can you identify what it is? There are two clues to the problem—one in the second paragraph and one in the third paragraph.

What does Andrew decide to do to try and solve the problem?

Slowly the wood took shape. When Andrew had finished, he held in his hands a smooth, new baseball bat. It was a nice bat, made of hickory. It would work well to teach his comrades to play the game, Andrew decided.

With the bat swinging lazily at his side, Andrew started across the field and approached the men who were still tossing around the old rawhide ball.

"Have any of you ever played baseball?" Andrew asked.

The men said they had never heard of the game, and looked quizzically at the bat in Andrew's left hand.

"Well," Andrew continued, "it's a game played with a bat like this and a ball just like the one you've been tossing back and forth."

The men appeared interested, so Andrew continued. They gathered around as he began scratching out a diagram of a baseball diamond in the dry earth, using a stick.

"The game is played by dividing into two teams," he said. "This is home plate," Andrew told them, as he drew a diamond in the dirt.

"Each team takes turns sending one player at a time to home plate to bat." Andrew motioned to the baseball bat he had laid on the ground next to him.

Next he drew three more diamonds. "Each of these is a base. There are three bases in addition to home plate," he said.

"The pitcher stands here." He drew a circle where the pitcher's mound would be. "The rest of the team spreads out in the field, leaving one man to guard each base."

"Guard it against what?" a young private asked.

"Good question," Andrew said. "I'm coming to that."

He continued, "The pitcher throws the ball to the man at home plate, who tries to hit it with the bat." Again, Andrew motioned to the bat he had made.

"Each batter gets three chances to hit the ball. If he misses all three times, he is out. If he hits the ball, he must run safely to a base before being tagged with the ball."

Andrew turned his attention to the young man who had asked the question about guarding bases.

"The players in the field don't want the batter to make it to base. Their goal is to get the ball to the man guarding the base before the batter reaches it. If you are successful in getting the ball to the base before the batter arrives, that batter is out," Andrew said.

Andrew took the time to explain how baseball is played to the men. What was their reaction? What two things did they hope playing baseball would do?

The men seemed to like the idea of the game Andrew was explaining, and this made him very happy. Playing games of baseball would help pass the time more quickly, and maybe take their minds off the heat.

"Once three people on a team strike out, or are tagged out, the teams trade places. The team that was batting goes into the field, and the team from the field comes in to bat."

The men were now smiling and whispering excitedly to one another. Baseball sounded fun. Andrew stopped to answer some questions.

"How many players are on a team?"

"Who decides if the pitches are good or bad?" they wanted to know.

Andrew patiently explained that teams should be divided evenly, with nine members of each team playing at a time. He went on to tell them that a man called an *umpire* was in charge of deciding whether pitches were good or bad.

By this time, the men were anxious to give the game of baseball a try. They divided into teams and set up a makeshift field, using burlap bags for bases.

The first game was indeed a sight to see. The players didn't have baseball gloves, so catching the ball hurt their hands. Several men attempted to hold the bat at the wrong end, and Andrew had to step in to correct them.

Was the captain a good umpire? Why or why not?

The captain of the unit was recruited to be the umpire, but did not prove to be a very good one, as he did not understand the rules of the game.

Eventually, however, the games began to run smoothly. Tents were moved out of the way, and right in the middle of camp, a primitive baseball field emerged.

Andrew was a very good player. He was a good batter and an even better pitcher. However, there was something else special about Andrew; he was left-handed. In fact, Andrew was such a good left-handed pitcher and batter, that the other men nicknamed him "The Southpaw."

What was special about Andrew aside from the fact that he was a good baseball player? Because of this what did the other men in his unit do? What was the nickname they gave him? A southpaw is someone who is left-handed. Knowing this, do you think The Southpaw was a good nickname for Andrew?

Andrew never missed a pitch. He hit everything the pitcher threw at him and was quick on his feet. It was almost impossible to catch him once he took off for a base.

When he was in the field, he struck out almost every batter! Nobody could hit Andrew's fastball.

By teaching the men in his unit to play baseball, did Andrew help solve the two problems we identified at the beginning of the story?

Did the soldiers of the Civil War enjoy baseball? Why did baseball become more popular and widely played during the Civil War?

The men loved watching him pitch. They thought he looked funny as he wound up for a pitch, wrinkling his face in concentration before releasing the ball.

Baseball became so popular among the men in Andrew's unit that they gave themselves team names, and even tried to organize games with other units when they could.

Andrew had been right, playing baseball helped fill the long days. It also gave the men something to think about other than the heat and the war. He and his unit spent many hours playing baseball, and they weren't the only ones.

People like Andrew were sharing the game of baseball in units across both the North and the South. It grew in popularity, and even after the end of the war, people continued to play. Baseball was on its way to becoming a favorite American pastime.

5 Assess Understanding

1. Distribute copies of the graphic organizer.

2. Tell the students to listen to the selection again and make notes or draw pictures to help them remember what happened in the story.

3. Reread the selection.

Baseball

Remembering My Youth, Through Baseball

NON FICTION

LESSON MAP

1 Getting Started.

2 Read the selection to the group.

3 Present the graphic organizer.

4 Read the selection to the group while working with them to use the graphic organizer.

5 Assess understanding.

MATERIALS

Graphic Organizer #4—Facts and Feelings/Opinions: displayed on an overhead; a copy for each student

Related Web sites: http://www.npr.org/templates/story/story.php?storyId=4968507

1 Getting Started

BACKGROUND

1. Explain that students will be listening to a radio commentary from October 2005, "Remembering My Youth, Through Baseball," by Mark Anthony Neal.

2. There are several types of commentaries; this one is a personal narrative. The author is expressing his thoughts and feelings about people in baseball who affected his life. This type of commentary is informal and not always tied tightly together.

3. Before students listen to the selection, encourage them to share basic information about baseball. Make sure they know what the World Series is and that Roberto Clemente, Willie Mays, Reggie Jackson, Daryl Strawberry, and Barry Bonds were some of the most dynamic and important players in baseball.

VOCABULARY

Present the vocabulary words, using this format:

Conjures is a verb that means **calls up or brings back.** What is **conjures?** *Conjures is a verb that means calls up or brings back.*

Listen. **The smell of popcorn conjures memories of going to the movies.** Say that. *The smell of popcorn conjures memories of going to the movies.*

majestic *adjective,* royal, grand. *The majestic statue of Lincoln filled the room.*

full-fledged *adjective,* full grown, experienced. *When I got my driver's license, I felt like a full-fledged driver.*

personified *verb, illustrated, showed. Superman personified strength.*

metaphor *noun, symbol, sign. A four-leaf clover is a metaphor for good luck.*

2 Read the Selection

1. The first reading should be presented with minimal interruption. If a student does ask a question, answer it and continue reading.

2. After presenting the selection, present the graphic organizer.

3 Present the Graphic Organizer

1. Display the graphic organizer, and discuss it briefly. Point out that a fact is information we can check. For example, We can check the dates of the 1959 World Series. However, the statement 'The New York Mets make people happy' is an opinion. The Mets don't make everyone happy, and we can't prove that they do.

2. Explain to the students that they will work through the organizer with you.

4 Use the Graphic Organizer

Read the selection in sections, and ask the students to tell you a fact or an opinion in each section. If necessary, model the thinking process. Suggestions are with the selection.

Write the information on your organizer.

Facts and Feelings/Opinions

This graphic organizer works well for distinguishing between facts and opinions.

Facts:

1. (Answers may vary.) The Orioles played the Pirates in the 1971 World Series.
2. Roberto Clemente hit a home run during the game against the Orioles.
3. In 1973, Willie Mays was 42 and in his last season.
4. Reggie Jackson played in the 1973 World Series.
5.

Feelings/Opinions:

1. The most important thing about fall is the Fall Classic in baseball.
2. Roberto Clemente was a majestic athlete.
3. Willie Mays personified grace.
4. During the 1973 Series, Reggie Jackson exuded brashness.
5.

Remembering My Youth, Through Baseball

by Mark Anthony Neal

ED GORDON, host: (from October 21, 2005) The World Series kicks off tomorrow in Chicago. Both teams already have a big reason to celebrate. For the Houston Astros, it's their first trip to the World Series. The Chicago White Sox have only done slightly better. Their last World Series visit was in 1959. But no matter who's playing on Saturday, commentator and baseball fan Mark Anthony Neal says there's no way he'd miss the big game.

Listen for an opinion. For example, how Neal feels about autumn. Here's a fact: the date of the Orioles/Pirates series. How can we prove that?

MARK ANTHONY NEAL: Perhaps no other season of the year is as endearing to me than autumn. Sure, I dig things like apple picking, fall foliage in the Adirondacks, and that hint of coolness in the air that allows you to rock that cable knit sweater. But most importantly, it's time for the Fall Classic: baseball's World Series. Indeed, the World Series conjures memories of my childhood and my understanding of the manhood that awaited. I was only five years old when I watched my first World Series. It was 1971 and the Baltimore Orioles were battling the burly Pittsburgh Pirates.

(Soundbite of 1971 World Series game)
Unidentified Sports Announcer: Pirates lead 1–nothing, playing here in the top of the fourth. Each team in with one hit.

NEAL: It was that series that introduced me to the majestic athleticism of Roberto Clemente, a whirling blur of speed and style who became one of the sport's dominant Latino stars. For years after first watching Clemente, whenever I played softball I would purposely wear my hat loosely on my head so that it would fall off the same way that Clemente's did as he rounded the bases.

(Soundbite of 1971 World Series game)
Unidentified Sports Announcer: Here's Bobby Clemente. Pops to short his first time up. Hits a screwball a mile into left-center field. It is going, it is gone!
(Soundbite of cheering crowd)

Neal compares Willie Mays and Reggie Jackson. This is the essence of the commentary: The author expresses his feelings and opinions about facts in such a way that it is difficult for a listener to separate them. It is much easier to do that when reading.

Here Neal summarizes his thoughts.

NEAL: By 1973, I was a full-fledged baseball fanatic, and it was my favorite team, the New York Mets, playing the Oakland A's for the World Series title. Though the Mets lost, my enduring memory of that series was the performances of two players who were at opposite ends of their careers. Throughout his career, Willie Mays personified grace, with a boyish charm that appealed to millions. But at 42 years old and in his last season, Mays tripped and slipped his way through the Series, becoming a metaphor for players who stayed in the game well past their primes. Indeed, Mays' performance helped my seven-year-old self better understand the ravages of aging. In comparison, Reggie Jackson had yet to reach his peak. That would come a few years later when he joined the New York Yankees and became Mr. October. But during the 1973 Series, Jackson exuded the brashness that would later become synonymous with him and generations of black ball players who would come after him, including Daryl Strawberry and Barry Bonds.

As I approach the age of 40 and begin to contemplate the realities of middle age, watching baseball has become one of the ways that I tap into a youthfulness that I hope will travel with me well into my senior years. Decades later, Roberto Clemente, Willie Mays, and Reggie Jackson remain dear to me, if only because they gave me a glimpse into the range of possibilities that awaited a little nappy-headed black boy who simply loved to watch baseball.

GORDON: Mark Anthony Neal is an associate professor with the Department of African and African American Studies at Duke University and author of *The New Black Man.*

This is NPR News.

⑤ Assess Understanding

1. Distribute copies of the graphic organizer.

2. Tell the students to listen to the selection again and make notes to help them remember some of the facts and the opinions.

3. Reread the selection.

Story Elements

This graphic organizer works well for identifying the elements of a short story and often the elements of a short nonfiction narrative.

Setting

Time:	Place:

Characters

Problem

Climax

Resolution

Character Qualities

This graphic organizer works well for describing a character and giving examples of a character's personality. It may be used for fiction or nonfiction.

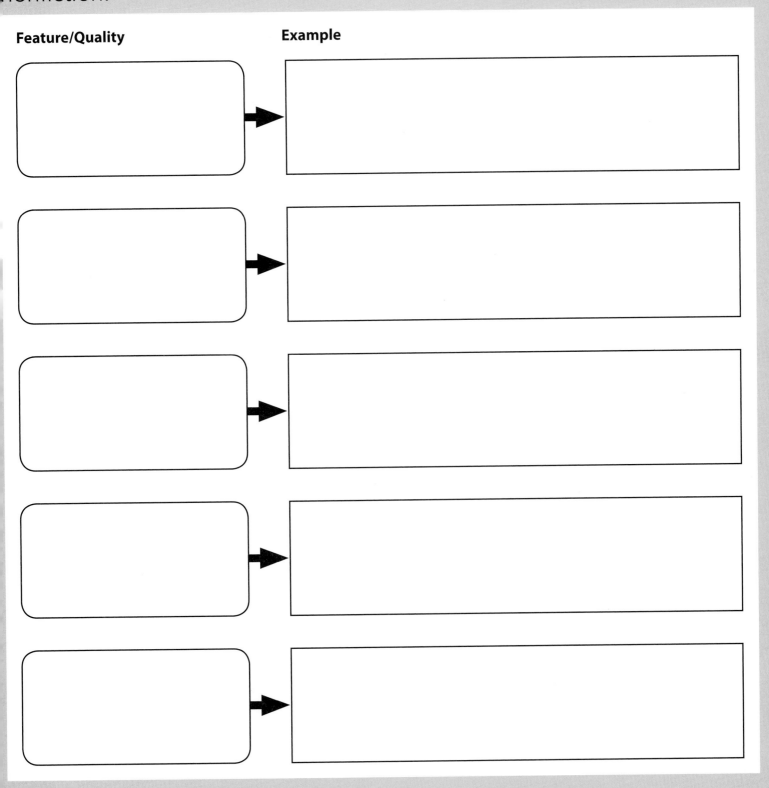

Feature/Quality

Example

Chain of Events

This graphic organizer works well for showing the steps in a process, tracing the plot of a story, and recording the sequence of an event.

Facts and Feelings/Opinions

This graphic organizer works well for distinguishing between facts and opinions.

Facts:

1.

2.

3.

4.

5.

Feelings/Opinions:

1.

2.

3.

4.

5.

Cause and Effect

This graphic organizer works well for showing simple cause and effect. By adding relationship arrows, you can also use it to show a chain of cause and effect, multiple effects from a single cause, or multiple causes with a single effect.

Cause (Why)

Effect (What)

Cluster Diagram

This type of organizer is a good way to show information that is related by topic but not by hierarchy; for example, questions and answers about a class of animals.

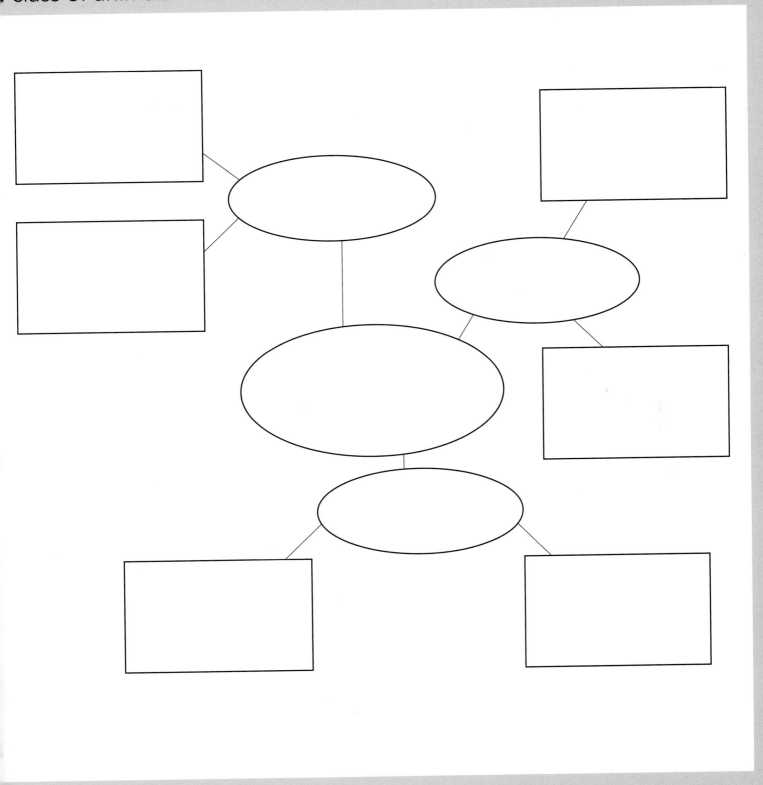